'With the Palestinians repudiated by the United States under President Trump this desperate, oppressed and occupied people needs friends. Palestinians face an Apartheid-existence under a Greater Israel. And they must feel the world has turned its back on this tragic plight. The more remarkable that an Australian man chose to walk the roads to dramatize their case. This principled and thoughtful citizen, John Salisbury, records in diary form his encounters and reflections along the way. This is a book with a very Australian character and a strong message of social justice, respecting the rights of a suffering people determined not to be airbrushed from existence.'

The Hon Bob Carr
Retired Australian politician who served as Premier of New South Wales from 1995 to 2005, as the leader of the Labor Party, and later served as Minister for Foreign Affairs from 2012 to 2013.

'John Salisbury's Walk for Palestine is the engaging story of an Anglo Australian man's journey – both literal and metaphorical – from being an uncritical supporter of Israel to being a passionate activist for the rights and dignity of the Palestinian people. As he walks hundreds of kilometres through the roads and paddocks of regional Australia collecting signatures, John finds overwhelming support for the Palestinian cause: fairness is something Australians instinctively understand. John's Walk for Palestine shows that every act in support of justice is a step in the right direction for the world.'

Melissa Parke
UN human rights expert and former Australian Labor Party politician who served as Member of the Australian Parliament (MP) Fremantle. Parke served as Minister for International Development in 2013.

'It is necessary, but a challenge, to walk a single mile in the shoes of the marginalised and oppressed. John Salisbury has walked not one but thousands in solidarity with the indigenous people of Palestine; victims not simply of Zionist ambition for their land and homes, but of western silence in the face of this gross injustice and oppression. Join his voice and stand up for human rights and the imposition of international law as you read this, his remarkable story.'

George Browning
9th bishop of the Diocese of Canberra and Goulburn
in the Anglican Church of Australia.

'A powerfully articulated journey into the light of resistance. Salisbury takes us on a trail illuminated by one man's quest for justice and human rights. His final words are a call to action and a reminder that we can make a difference.'

Samah Sabawi
Palestinian playwright, author and poet. Policy advisor to the Palestinian policy network Al-Shabaka, and a member of the board of directors of the National Council on Canada-Arab Relations.

WALKING

FOR

PALESTINE

JOHN SALISBURY

ISBN: 978-0-646-81882-5   eISBN: 978-1-922270-27-6

 NATIONAL LIBRARY OF AUSTRALIA
A catalogue record for this book is available from the National Library of Australia

Dedicated to the many children of Gaza, who, maimed by Israeli sniper bullets, will never walk again.

For Wendy.
The love of my life and such a
contributor to this project.

Contents

Foreword

Supporting the Palestinian cause can be a lonely pursuit. My first recollections of doing so was when I was a teenager, raised in Melbourne as a secular Jew in the 1980s, and I constantly heard harsh denunciations of then Palestinian leader Yasser Arafat ("terrorist!", "murderer!", "the new Hitler!" etc) and refusal to even accept the fact that Israel was occupying Palestinian territory.

My knowledge of the conflict was minimal back then, in the years before the internet it was much harder to know the exact realities of Israel's brutal occupation of the West Bank, East Jerusalem and Gaza, but I remember feeling uncomfortable with the knee-jerk Jewish contempt for the Palestinian issue. I either remained silent or pushed back against Jewish tribalism. Many in my family were less than impressed.

Fast forward to the years after September 11, 2001 and arguing for the rights of Palestinians for self-determination was not a popular cause. When I released my first book, *My Israel Question*, in 2006, there were various attempts to censor it – the Israel lobby harassed my publisher and the university behind it, Melbourne University Press, in attempts to get the book pulped – and Jewish MPs denounced me in parliament (both before and after the book was out).

Now, years later, living in occupied East Jerusalem, I rarely think about those experiences (though they certainly forced me to grow a very thick skin as I had to deal with constant hate mail and death threats). Today, the Palestinian cause has never been more supported across the globe, from France to Australia and the UK to Spain, and yet on the ground across Palestine the situation has never been grimmer. With over 750,000 Jewish squatters living illegally on Palestinian land, and the Trump administration giving unqualified support to Israeli apartheid in the West Bank, East Jerusalem and Gaza, Palestinians are forced to resist and just survive.

It may seem incredibly strange for an Australian man like John to support the Palestinian cause but in fact it's anything but. Like previous struggles for justice in East Timor and South Africa, John knows the importance of solidarity with oppressed peoples, no matter how difficult it is to get our political leaders to understand and listen. His Walking for Palestine is a compelling roadmap for citizens who ask what just one person can do to help the Palestinian issue. His commitment, time and strength is inspiring because it's the exact opposite of what most Australians do on a daily basis. History remembers people like John because they want their voices to be heard and refuse to be cowered by false allegations of anti-Semitism. John shows up because the cause is just.

I like how John explains his journey towards Palestine solidarity. He's not a "quiet Australian", head down and disinterested in other people's struggles, but open, angry, public and dogged in his pursuit of raising the profile of the Palestinian push for independence and dignity.

I thank John for his inclusion of my work. The only way Palestine will be free is through a combination of local and global forces coming together and saying that the longest occupation in modern history is no longer acceptable. It's heartening to think that people like John will be part of that action.

Antony Loewenstein
East Jerusalem, January 2020

Antony Loewenstein is a Jerusalem-based Australian journalist who has written for *The New York Times*, *The Guardian*, the BBC, *The Washington Post*, *The Nation*, *Huffington Post*, *Haaretz*, and many others. His latest book is *Pills, Powder and Smoke: Inside the Bloody War on Drugs*. He's the author of *Disaster Capitalism: Making a Killing Out of Catastrophe*; the writer/co-producer of the associated documentary, *Disaster Capitalism*; and the co-director of an Al-Jazeera English film on the opioid drug tramadol. His other books include *My Israel Question*, *The Blogging Revolution*, and *Profits of Doom*, and he is the co-editor of the books *Left Turn* and *After Zionism*, and is a contributor to *For God's Sake*. He's been reporting on Israel/Palestine since 2003.

Preface

Why would a 60-year-old man with an Anglo-Saxon heritage set out on a series of long distance walks in support of the Palestinian cause?

What motivated him and what was achieved?

If you have even a passing interest in the unresolved issue of Palestine, then this book is for you.

This book is about journeys. Physical journeys, to be sure, but also those of the moral and intellectual variety.

The physical journeys for Palestinian rights that clocked well over a thousand kilometres took place over the course of four years: 2014, 2015, 2016 and 2018. The other journeys were longer. Those took several decades. One of them was the crossing from one side of the debate to the other – the path that led to finally and irrevocably taking sides with the oppressed and determining to do something about it. The physical journeys were preceded by those of the mind and heart. Without them, not a single step would have been taken.

In this vein, I need to first outline what happened to me intellectually before I began my walks for Palestine. There is no specific start date, not a single event on a single day. Rather, it was a slow and gradual build-up of events that encouraged a change of mind.

The Plight of Global Jewry and International Sympathy

MANY OF US STARTED OUT AS SUPPORTERS OF ISRAEL. IT WAS easy to be that way after the awful events of Europe in the 1940s. The tragedy of the Holocaust and centuries of discrimination. Who could deny a safe place for a perennially persecuted people? It was eminently reasonable. The first time I was aware of Israel was via the movie Exodus starring Paul Newman. It was the screen adaptation of Leon Uris's bestselling book. I'm not sure how many people saw the film, but 55 million copies of the book have been sold, so it was a phenomenally popular book. Hollywood gave it the full treatment. It was a cracking yarn and it left one firmly in admiration of the Jewish people's struggle for security and a homeland. It was just what the young country needed to convince many of us about the justice of supporting it.

Re-reading the novel in 2018, in light of all that has happened subsequently, is illuminating. Uris's book is nothing but a relentless paean to the various Jewish militias associated with 1940s Palestine. As groups such as Haganah, Irgun and Lehi saw it, the occupier – Britain – needed to be removed by violence (so ironic in view of subsequent events). Uris is full of praise for the brave and resourceful militants who were regarded as terrorists by Great Britain. Each chapter is headed up with a biblical quotation such as Deuteronomy 1:8 – 'Go and possess the land which Jehovah swore unto your fathers, to Abraham, to Isaac and to Jacob. Give unto them and to their seed after them.' The author himself gives us lines such as, 'It was the army of Israel and no force on earth could stop them for the power of God was with them!' and 'Israel stands today as the greatest single instrument for bringing the Arab people out of the Dark Ages.'

The British, who had control of Palestine from 1920 under a League of Nations mandate, are portrayed by Uris as incompetent. The indigenous Arab population is consistently portrayed as being barbaric and uncivilised. Most concerning, all of the violence inflicted on the Arab and British people is justified by Uris as a means to an end. There is no attempt at presenting an unbiased, balanced view and it is factually sloppy, despite its presentation as a historical text. No matter. The author would have been well pleased with the result: young impressionable minds were won over to the cause throughout the world.

The next time Israel appeared on my 'radar screen' would have been in 1967. I was barely a teenager but the impression was, once again, of a triumph for the brave young nation. The Six-Day War of 1967 saw one small nation pitted against several larger ones: Egypt, Syria and Jordan. This time, David slew three Goliaths in record-breaking time. Arab humiliation followed and the victor told the story. We were still young and naïve; Israel had the endorsement of nearly all of us in the West.

My next memory of Israel is from the 1970s. During this time, it became fashionable to spend a few months in Israel living in a kibbutz. This became quite popular with Antipodeans travelling to and from Europe. Living on a kibbutz meant you were clothed, fed and housed in return for your labour. Its structure of communal living was appealing to many looking for a possible alternative to capitalism. One of my closest friends spent three months at Mefalsim Kibbutz near the Gaza Strip. He enjoyed it. Circumstances, not conviction, meant I did not visit a kibbutz myself. I, like most, was not acquainted with the situation for Palestinians in those days.

Whether or not it was deserved, there seems to have been quite a lot of support for Israel in those days.

The capture of Israeli Athletes at the 1972 Munich Olympic Games may have been the first time that the Israel/Palestine issue hit Western newspapers and television screens in a big way. The Palestinian terror group Black September took eleven Israeli athletes hostage. A rescue mission failed and both the hostages and perpetrators were killed. It was awful. Not much, if any, thought was given to anything by way of historical background. The media coverage was relentless in depicting the horror of the terrorism but not what had caused it. Understanding the bigger historical picture of this land in the Middle East would have to wait several more years. For now, it was, once again, sympathy for a country that apparently endured unprovoked attacks.

Victimisation of the Palestinians

P<small>ERHAPS THE FIRST INSTANCE OF</small> I<small>SRAEL'S AGGRESSIVE</small> militarism, for me, came with the notorious massacres at the Sabra and Shatila refugee camps in 1982. Although the slaughter of up to 3500 Palestinian civilians was carried out by Lebanese Christian Phalangist militia, they were assisted and encouraged by the Israel Defense Forces under General Ariel Sharon. Newspaper articles by the likes of Robert Fisk conveyed some deeply disturbing facts. I was beginning to worry. After all, it didn't feel much like the Munich incident of ten years earlier. I was not sure what to think but pushed my concerns to one side. At the time, there were other international injustices, like the Indonesian occupation and annexation of East Timor, that preoccupied me more. During the 1980s I joined Amnesty International. Membership meant receiving a regular publication that drew attention to human rights abuses around the globe. Israel was often included in the pages of that publication. Slowly but surely many of us were changing our minds.

The Israeli victory in the Six-Day War of 1967 was swift and clear-cut but had other long-term consequences. Under Article Four of the Geneva Convention 1949 it is illegal to move your population onto land acquired as a result of war. Israel, however, did just that and continues to. The UN Partition Plan of 1947 recommended 56% of Mandatory Palestine to be apportioned for Israel. The Palestinians, not unnaturally, thought the division unfair. After all, they outnumbered the Jewish (mostly refugees from Europe) population by more than 2 to 1. Following hostilities in 1948, Israeli control extend to 78% of the total land area. Since 1967,

Israel has controlled 100% of the land. This control has endured despite numerous UN resolutions condemning it. Somehow, only insignificant objections to this occupation seemed to manifest themselves in Australian media coverage during the '70s, '80s and '90s. We witnessed year after year of negotiations and 'peace talks' that were supposed to bring about resolution to the conflict. All ended without progress.

Along with the occupation of the West Bank by Israeli soldiers, there was another matter of concern: illegal settlements. We began to understand the full nature of the 1967 Six-Day War when illegal Jewish-only settlements began to be built in the only area left for a Palestinian state: the West Bank and the Gaza Strip. The settlements began in a trickle but the intermittent trickle became a steady stream.

The general blasé approach to the Israel/Palestine question was becoming difficult to sustain. Permanent-looking Jewish housing estates were being built in the midst of areas clearly thought of by the world as part of a future Palestinian state. The issue had plenty of media coverage. Every American president from Jimmy Carter onwards would solemnly declare that they would be the one to fix the problem. Endless rounds of negotiations got nowhere. In 1987, Palestinians staged an anti-occupation uprising (the First Intifada). It looked awful. Of course, the death toll of Palestinians to Israelis was in the ratio of at minimum 10:1. The Intifada went on for six years and resulted in the Oslo Accords. The Israelis skilfully manipulated the airwaves, newspapers and television screens to make it look like they were the victims, not the instigators, of the mess. Joris Luyendijk wrote an excellent book on the Israeli media machine – *Fit to Print*. Then something extraordinary happened: Israeli Prime Minister Yitzhak Rabin was assassinated.

It was 1995. The Oslo Accords had been signed by Rabin and Palestinian leader Yasser Arafat. I didn't fully realise it at the time, but the Oslo Accords were never designed to lead to any sort of Palestinian state. Or at least any sort of *viable* Palestinian state.

Nonetheless, Rabin was assassinated for being part of the deal. But not by a Palestinian, by an Israeli! The full extent of the unholy mess was unfolding for the world to see. Far from the heroic and brave characters that were portrayed in Leon Uris's book, right-wing religious fanatics like Yigal Amir were prepared to kill their own leader for their messianic religious ideas. Theocratic nationalism was now clearly part of this conflict. My views were changed. Some Jewish Israelis believed that all the land between the Jordan River and the Mediterranean had been given to them by God. These Israelis were dismissive of any UN resolutions. They were also dismissive of rulings by the International Court of Justice. And they had complete disregard for the Geneva Conventions signed in 1949. They used the Bible as justification for everything. And, they put their faith in overwhelming military superiority. By now, they had lost me. I started to realise the true nature of the situation.

The next round of futile 'peace talks' was held at Camp David in 2000. President Bill Clinton was keen to achieve something positive at the end of his eight-year presidency. Once again, we saw the media follow the negotiations intently. Once again, the discussions were between an intransigent Goliath and a hapless David. For peace to occur, Israel would have to make concessions. But, from their position of overwhelming strength, why should they? At any rate, from the Palestinian point of view, what was there to talk about? Israel was the party in violation of UN resolutions and International Court of Justice rulings. Just comply. Just withdraw. Of course, Israel would do no such thing. They offered token gestures (not in writing) but suggested that Palestine make concessions too. It is a popular misconception that Arafat was the intransigent party to the talks. However, one of the chief Israeli diplomats at Camp David, Shlomo Ben-Ami, said years later, 'If I were a Palestinian, I would have rejected Camp David as well.'

All of the historical events mentioned above are part of the drip, drip, drip that led to my reversal of initial support for Israel into outright opposition. The failure of the Camp David talks in 2001 saw Palestinian frustration boil over. A Second Intifada took place. For some Palestinians, suicide bombers became the tactic of choice. Extremely gruesome but what was the cause? Israeli historian Benny Morris shed some light when describing the causes of the Intifada. He said that there was an 'all pervading element of humiliation' caused by the protracted occupation that was 'always a brutal and mortifying experience for the occupied [...] founded on brute force, repression and fear, collaboration and treachery, beatings and torture chambers, and daily intimidation, humiliation and manipulation' (*Righteous Victims: A History of the Zionist-Arab Conflict, 1881–2001*, Vintage, pp. 341, 568).

Some serious political and academic voices were giving weight to our suspicions that Israel was not the innocent party to the conflict. Israeli historian Avi Schlaim spoke about the mass expulsion of Palestinians in 1948 and the destruction of 400 Palestinian villages. He said, 'Whichever way you look at it, the creation of the state of Israel in 1948 involved a monumental injustice.' In 2006, former American President Jimmy Carter also wrote a book about the situation. It was entitled *Palestine: Peace Not Apartheid*. Carter was not uncritical about Israel's approach. The book was a bestseller but resulted in the wrath of Hades being rained down upon Carter by the pro-Israel community in America. Criticism of Israel would be countered swiftly. This swift criticism of any voice critical of the Israeli government became an ongoing part of the issue. Namely, that Israel and its supporters realised that they needed to carry out long and persistent campaigns to counter any negative representation of their crimes in the conflict. Even though your case was weak you could counter the facts by excoriating those brave enough to state them.

In 1947 the UN recommended partition of British-controlled Mandatory Palestine. 56% was to be for Israel and 44% for Palestine. Part of the area recommended for Palestine included the

Gaza Strip. Many of the Palestinian refugees who fled Israel in 1948 ended up as refugees in Gaza. After the Six-Day War in 1967, Gaza was occupied, just as the West Bank was, by Israel. Eight thousand Jewish settlers built houses there. A blatant violation of the Geneva Convention. Up to 25% of the tiny land area was set aside for them. Imagine that ratio when 1.8 million Palestinians lived in the strip. In 2003, a young International Solidarity Movement activist from America was in the Gaza Strip protesting the demolition of Palestinian houses. Her name was Rachel Corrie. She was knocked over and killed by an Israeli armoured bulldozer. Her death and the subsequent fruitless striving for justice by her parents became a cause célèbre. Her heroism has been a huge inspiration for me and I will talk about her more later in this book.

In 2005, whilst George Bush Junior attempted to 'fix' the Middle East problem, elections were held for a Palestinian President. Mahmoud Abbas was elected. Then the American president urged Israeli Prime Minister Ariel Sharon to withdraw from the Gaza Strip both soldiers and settlers. It is often trumpeted as a very generous gesture that Sharon did as George Bush asked. However, one has to ask, what on earth were they doing there in the first place? In any case the settlers simply relocated to the West Bank. In January 2006, more elections were held in Palestine. Palestinians in the Gaza Strip and the West Bank voted for members of the Palestinian Legislative Council. Unfortunately, the results of the election meant that Hamas won. That did not suit George Bush or Israel so the results were abandoned and ignored. Instead, a blockade and siege were inflicted on the people of Gaza by Israel. Even now as I write these words the blockade continues.

The Australian Perspective

In 2006 I read a book entitled *My Israel Question*, by a young Jewish Australian writer named Antony Loewenstein. I was amazed to read of his experiences. He first became involved in the matter of Israel in 2003, following the awarding of the Sydney Peace Prize to Christian Palestinian woman Hanan Ashrawi. Some sections of the Sydney and Melbourne Jewish community were upset with the decision and embarked on a furious campaign to have the decision reversed. Pressure was applied on New South Wales Premier at the time Bob Carr. He stood firm. Financial pressure was then directed on the Sydney Peace Prize organising committee through sponsors.

Loewenstein was embarrassed to see the pro-Israel lobby behaving so vehemently against the recipient of the award. He wrote an article in the *Sydney Morning Herald* entitled, 'Defiant Israel Blind to What It Has Become.' He outlined the brutality of the ongoing occupation, the suffering of the Palestinians and the apparent Jewish acceptance of the situation. Loewenstein relates how, as a result of this article, he received a 'barrage of vitriol' from fellow members of the Jewish community. Sadly, he and his parents were gradually ostracised from former friends and even some family members because of his writing. Speaking out came at a price. The conversations, and letters and emails he received, criticising his piece were 'marked by a blind devotion to the state of Israel and a desperate need to justify its actions.' He said, 'It seemed to me that nationalism had become something beyond religion for too many

Jews. Devotion to the state of Israel, sacred and beyond criticism, had become central to contemporary Jewish thought.'

Loewenstein's book made a deep impression on me. As well as outlining his own personal journey the author goes back into a brief history of Zionism and the creation of Israel. He also draws a wide arc picture of the state of Israel today. He demonstrates clearly the enthusiasm with which Jewish neo-conservatives proselytised for the 2003 Iraq War. He even predicted the present day determination to work for regime change in Iran. I highly recommend reading Loewenstein's book.

As I was reading about the attempts to reverse the decision on awarding the 2003 Sydney Peace Prize and the nasty campaign inflicted on Antony Loewenstein, I discovered that these were hardly isolated incidents. Even Steven Spielberg was castigated for his 2005 film *Munich* because the film seemed to 'equate the Israeli assassins with "terrorists"' and the film 'prefers a discussion of counter-terrorism to a discussion of terrorism; or it thinks that they are the same discussion'. The film did demonstrate the lengths that Israel would go to in order to eliminate its enemies. Always prioritise vengeance over forgiveness.

In 2007 I read another book demonstrating Israel's nefarious activities, called *Kill Khalid* (subtitled *Mossad's Failed Hit...and the Rise of Hamas*) by Australian journalist Paul McGeough. The book is a fascinating exposé on the work of Israel's spy agency Mossad. Taking out enemies, it turns out, is an Israeli speciality and the book is about an attempt to assassinate Khalid Mishal in Amman, Jordan, in 1997. Posing as Canadian tourists, the Mossad agents accosted the Hamas leader in broad daylight in downtown Amman, injecting an unknown chemical into his ear. Had it been successful, the victim should have felt no pain but be dead within 48 hours. The plan failed. The Mossad agents' escape plans were botched. They were arrested and detained in a Jordanian jail. Medical advice indicated that the Palestinian Mishal was slowly dying. Israel, under pressure from Jordan's King Hussein and even then American President Bill Clinton, was forced to provide the poison antidote. Khalid Mishal lived. The book is a fascinating read. The incident provides yet another example of an extrajudicial killing being carried out with expected immunity from sanction. It is worth noting that Khalid Mishal was a democratically elected representative of the Palestinian people.

In 2010, Australian passports were used by Mossad for up to 33 agents entering Dubai to complete another assassination. The target this time was Hamas figure Mahmoud al-Mabhouh. Because Israel stole the identities of real Australian citizens, there was a diplomatic protest by Australia at the time. An Israeli diplomat was expelled by the Rudd Government. However, it was relatively muted. Especially compared to the very strong outrage expressed by our Foreign Minister Julie Bishop for Russia's alleged poisoning of double agent Sergei Skripal in Salisbury, England, in 2018.

In February 2018, Israeli author Ronen Bergman released a book, *Rise and Kill First*, that provides a comprehensive synopsis of Israel's secret agencies. According to Bergman, Israel has assassinated more people than any other Western country since World War II, 2700 targeted killings from 1948 onwards. Some of the methods used include: poisoned toothpaste that takes a month to end its victim's life, exploding mobile phones, armed drones, spare tyres with remote control bombs, the assassination of enemy scientists, and discovering the secret lovers of Muslim clerics.

From the early 2000s it became literally impossible to ignore the negative effect Israel was having on global politics. Despite the international community having a lot of sympathy for Jewish people after World War II, that sympathy was being whittled away because of repeated violations of the international rules-based order. More and more people became convinced that an injustice of horrendous proportions was being systematically carried out against the Palestinians across several decades. Worse still, Israel was getting away with it.

In 2014, Australian journalist Peter Greste spent seven months in an Egyptian jail. He was arrested whilst working for Al Jazeera and charged with journalistic reporting that was 'damaging to national security'. He was on the ABC program *Q&A* in April 2015. The program's host, Tony Jones, had this discussion with him:

> Jones: 'Why are so many young Muslims, even from affluent families in Europe and other places, including Australia, why are they so attracted to ISIS?'
>
> Greste: 'This is one of the things. There's a lot of talk about how disaffected youth seem to be winding up in these places and I think that is a great myth. There is a sense, amongst the Islamic community, that Islam is under attack. Now I'm not suggesting that it is, I'm simply trying to explain the logic that a lot of these kids are adopting. There is a sense...'
>
> Jones: 'Do you think they have a point?'
>
> Greste: 'It's hard to disagree or not see their point of view. I mean they are incredibly angry with the way Muslims are treated by the Israelis. For example: the way that the West seems to be supporting Israel. They are incredibly angry at the way USA and its allies have behaved in Iraq and Afghanistan.'

It was a very telling point. Greste had spent a long time in an Egyptian jail, but rather than concentrate on his personal misfortune, he was addressing the broader issue of regional security. For Australia to support Israel so strongly was not in our best interests. We had very little trade with Israel. In 2015–16 Israel was Australia's 37th largest merchandise trading partner. Two-way goods and services trade amounted to $1.3 billion, of which

Australian exports were worth $349 million and imports from Israel were worth $952 million. It is a very modest figure. By contrast, the two-way merchandise trade with the United Arab Emirates is over $5 billion. China is by far our largest trading partner with two-way trade of over $150 billion. So our support for Israel was not because that country was vital to our financial security.

The Pro-Israel Perspective

I RESOLVED TO TRY AND UNDERSTAND THE ISRAELI perspective a little better, if at all possible. During 2014 I attended three lectures at the Jewish Centre for Civilisation at Monash University. On 21 May, the speaker was prominent Israeli journalist Ari Shavit. He had recently written a book entitled *My Promised Land: The Triumph and Tragedy of Israel*. He appeared to indicate, by using the word 'tragedy' in the title of his book, that something was wrong in the land of his birth. Other audience members may have been conscious of a potential problem too. However, his talk was mostly of the deep and abiding love he had for his homeland. He spoke glowingly of the old Israel, the Israel of the 1950s and 1960s, and he somehow pined for Israel to be that place again. Unsurprisingly, he did not offer any solution as to how to deal with the current realities of the occupation and ever-expanding settlements. Shortly after his visit, Shavit removed himself from public life, following accusations of inappropriate sexual conduct by two Jewish women.

The next speaker was Peter Beinart. Beinart spoke on 5 June. Once again, his visit was as part of a speaking tour following the release of his book *The Crisis of Zionism*. Like Shavit, Beinart was an engaging and accomplished speaker. He did not live in Israel but was a frequent visitor. He was not so ideologically blind that he could not see issues with the Zionist project. However, his love of Judaism meant that ultimately he would not move decisively enough to reform or even abandon the Zionist project. He was, however, in favour of boycotting goods made in the West Bank.

Nothing that these two men said, charming and erudite though they were, convinced me that my concerns about injustice inflicted on Palestinians were misplaced. In fact, they reinforced my strong misgivings about Israel.

The last lecture was on 23 July. This time the speaker was Yossi Klein Halevi. I may have been the sole non-Jewish person sitting in the crowd that night. He was by far the most unforgiving of the three men. Only somebody with the most blindly tribal perspective would welcome the uncompromising message he spoke. He insisted that the Jews were indigenous to the land between the Jordan River and the Mediterranean. He also asserted, when referring to the 'troubles', that settlements in the West Bank were not a problem or even an issue. Halevi's talk demonstrated a blind devotion to a Jewish perspective that verged on fanaticism.

The Horror of Gaza

HALEVI'S VISIT TO MELBOURNE CAME AT THE SAME TIME AS Israel engineered a third horrendous military campaign (Operation Protective Edge) on the determined but hapless people of Gaza. It lasted for six weeks. I will never forget those images of four Palestinian children killed whilst playing on the beach. I will never forget those pictures of the devastation of the Shujaiya neighbourhood in Gaza City. Barely imagined horrors were being inflicted upon people who had literally no way to escape. The Pentagon reported that 11 artillery battalions pumped 7000 high explosive shells into the Shujaiya neighbourhood over a period of 24 hours. Even American officers were shocked at the 'scale and lethality of the Israeli bombardment' (Mark Perry, 'Why Israel's Bombardment of Gaza Left Us Officers "Stunned"', Al Jazeera America, 27 August 2014).

During the six weeks of Operation Protective Edge, it was noticeable that amongst the political leadership of Australia barely a word of criticism was uttered against Israel. I heard Malcolm Turnbull (then the Minister for Communications) speak on ABC Radio's AM programme on 31 July (article by Katharine Murphy, *The Guardian*, 31 July 2014). He was basically endorsing the words of Israeli spokesman Mark Regev. Similar sentiments were expressed by Labor leader Bill Shorten (article by Dennis Altman, *The Conversation*, 8 September 2014). Siding with a bully was never encouraged by my parents but seemed to be fine with our political elite. Why? It came back to the pressure applied by the lobby that I had read about in Antony Loewenstein's book.

I went to pro-Palestinian rallies twice outside Melbourne City Library. Seldom, if ever, in my life did I go onto the streets to protest, but I was that upset about the situation in Gaza, I felt motivated to get on my feet. Even though it was only a block or two of downtown Melbourne, I was walking my first steps for Palestine.

The historical raging injustice of the issue was one thing. Another was the total disparity in military strength. I wrote to our Foreign Minister asking her to withdraw our Ambassador to Israel. I know it was a forlorn hope but I felt I needed to do something. Around the same time, notable *Sydney Morning Herald* journalist Mike Carlton was sacked for being insufficiently polite to those angry about his commentary on Israel's massacre of Palestinians. I was sufficiently angry with Fairfax over this matter that I decided to cancel my subscription to their newspaper, after being a loyal subscriber for more than 20 years. Around this time I also went to see a play called *Tales of a City by the Sea* by a Palestinian Australian playwright, Samah Sabawi. It told a love story with present day Gaza as its backdrop. It was terrific. Not only as a fine piece of theatre, but also as an insight into what life is like living under siege.

Coincidentally, at that time I was reading *Confessions of a Failed Finance Minister* by Peter Walsh, the Australian Finance Minister during the Hawke government. I was amazed to read Walsh writing that 'Hawke's subservience to the Jewish lobby, or more accurately, its Melbourne wing, caused the War Crimes Tribunal Bill to be introduced and later enacted'. Writing of the Bill, the former Finance Minister noted, 'Whatever moral force the argument for the Bill had was somewhat diluted by the contemporary behaviour of the Israeli army in Gaza and the West Bank.' Walsh, a noted plain speaker on people and issues, was Finance Minister from 1984 to 1990. The book I have quoted from was written in 1995. Clear evidence that the pro-Israel lobby was influential well before Antony Loewenstein documented his experiences in 2006.

As I have outlined here, the pretence of Israel for peace and a two-state solution was mostly if not always, a ruse. Let us consider Gaza. We are always quick to express our distaste for the 'dreaded' Hamas, but let us remember some salient facts. Firstly, the organisation was set up in 1987. Well after the 1967 Six-Day War that led to the total control of historic Palestine. Secondly, the creation of Hamas was partially funded and certainly encouraged by Israel itself. This was because Israel was worried about the secular Palestinian group Fatah, which until that time had a monopoly on Palestinian national ambitions, led by Yasser Arafat. Having embarked on a divide and rule strategy, Israel was horrified to learn that Hamas became the more difficult of the two groups to manage and control. Hence, the current demonisation of them. And lastly, Gaza is one of the most densely populated places on earth. Its 1.8 million inhabitants occupy a land area of just 365 square kilometres (41 kilometres long by 612 kilometres wide). Yet, the 8000 Israeli settlers who lived there took roughly 25% of the land. Prime Minister Ariel Sharon made the decision to evacuate Jewish settlers from Gaza in 2005. Violent scenes erupted as many of the settlers were extremely reluctant to vacate. Propagandists for Israel often mention the fact that settlers *did* evacuate Gaza and expect the world to laud their actions. However, one might well ask the question, what on earth were they doing there in the first place? Those settlers and the Israeli government, which funded and protected them, certainly did not have any qualms about crossing the 'border' into Gaza. They considered they had a God given right to be there. In 2018, during the 'Great March of Return', young Palestinian men from Gaza approached the 'border' of Israel only to be slaughtered by Israel Defense Forces snipers. There was some 'chutzpah' in those contrasting standards. At every turn, and no matter which way one observed it, the behaviour of Israel was impossible to support.

The 2014 Israeli war on Gaza (Operation Protective Edge) resulted in the deaths of 2251 Palestinians, including 500 children.

1000 children were left with permanent disabilities. 1700 homes were destroyed. 250,000 people were displaced. Water and electrical supplies were damaged. The United Nations estimates that very soon Gaza will be unliveable if nothing is done to ease the blockade. Yet we still hear the constant refrain that 'Israel has the right to defend itself'. In Australia, as noted by former Finance Minister Peter Walsh, there was a level of subservience to the Jewish lobby. This was not just in the Labor Party. In 2013 I came across a transcript of a speech delivered by the then Minister of Communications, Malcolm Turnbull, at Caulfield Hebrew Congregation in Melbourne. It was a hagiographic speech. It could have been written by one of the spokespersons of the Jewish audience he was addressing. It did not even mention the occupation or settlements.

At the time I wrote to the minister by email saying, 'Disappointed in the Ha'atzmaut breakfast speech. Way too fawning.'

He responded with, 'Dear John, I think the speech was appropriate given the remarkable achievements of Israel over the past 65 years. Malcolm.'

I replied, 'Dear Malcolm, those achievements at devastating cost to others. We should not be complicit, even in a peripheral way, to expropriation of land based on religious entitlement.'

Malcolm responded again, 'Thanks John, it is a little more complex than that, as you know.'

I left the conversation there. In hindsight, what I should have written, and I am sure Malcolm really knows, is that it is not complex. Just accept the rulings of the International Court of Justice. Just comply with the Fourth Geneva Convention. Just follow the United Nations resolutions. That is what we should demand of Israel in the same way we demand it of other rogue states.

Similarly, in 2012, the then Leader of the Opposition, Tony Abbott, made a speech at the Central Synagogue in Sydney. I quote him from that speech: 'When Israel is fighting for its very life, well, as far as I am concerned, Australians are Israelis. We are all Israelis in those circumstances.'

While Julia Gillard was Prime Minister, I also wrote to her about my concerns regarding the suffering of the Palestinian people. I wrote to her via the online portal. It is a privilege enjoyed by democracies that you can correspond directly 'with the leader'. The portal responds immediately with an assurance that your message has been received and that the PM will respond because all contact is replied to. However, several weeks went by and no response was forthcoming after my email to Gillard. Another repeat attempt to engage with the PM was similarly met with silence. I also wrote two letters by hand and posted those for good measure, thinking that they might elicit a response. I received no response. In 2013, Ms Gillard received the Jerusalem Prize – a prize awarded by various combined Zionist bodies in Australia. Past recipients include Bob Hawke and John Howard. The Jerusalem Prize is awarded to those who display 'staunch commitment and loyalty to Israel'. Why she too gave a free pass to Israel in spite of all we know about Israel's brutal treatment of the Palestinians remains a mystery to me.

As the reader will have noticed, my transition from being an uncritical admirer (à la Leon Uris) of the Zionist project, to a deeply concerned, but uninvolved, opponent of the project was now complete. My mental and emotional journey had been all-encompassing and transformative. One of the things that was most impressive about the issue for me was the number of Jewish people who spoke out against Israel's actions. Renowned figures such as Norman Finkelstein and Noam Chomsky repeatedly wrote articles highlighting Israel's aggression and they also frequently debated against the supporters of Israel in America. In Tel Aviv and Jerusalem, the historians Ilan Pappé and Shlomo Sand wrote books that put the lie to Leon Uris's fictional account about the creation of Israel. Amazingly, wise Jewish men of yore were speaking out too.

Sigmund Freud: 'I concede with sorrow that the baseless fanaticism of our people is in part to be blamed for the awakening of Arab distrust. I can raise no sympathy at all for the misdirected piety which transforms a piece of a Herodian wall into a national relic, thereby offending the feelings of the natives.'

Albert Einstein: 'The [Israeli] state idea is not according to my heart. I cannot understand why it is needed. It is connected with many difficulties and a narrow-mindedness. I believe it is bad.'

Erich Fromm: 'The claim of the Jews to the Land of Israel cannot be a realistic political claim. If all nations would suddenly claim territories in which their forefathers lived two thousand years ago, this world would be a madhouse.'

Primo Levi: 'Everyone has their Jews. For the Israelis, they are the Palestinians.'

In Australia too, there were several people willing to speak up and say 'not in my name'. Sometimes they banded together in their opposition to create solidarity movements like the Independent Australian Jewish Voices, the Australian Jewish Democratic Society, and Jews Against the Occupation Australia. These groups are very significant, although they are small and tend to be from left-wing political orientations. That brought back memories of the campaign to end South Africa's apartheid. Activism often seems to begin in the left.

The First Walk

ALL OF THESE THOUGHTS WERE RUNNING AROUND IN MY brain when one day in September 2014 I noticed a post on Facebook by my now friend Antony Loewenstein. He was notifying his many Facebook followers of a walk from Sydney to Canberra for Palestinian solidarity. The walk was being undertaken by a Jewish Israeli academic, Dr Marcelo Svirsky. Marcelo was putting a call out to those interested to join him. Being a self-funded retiree, and in reasonable physical condition, I could not think of a reason not to join him.

At the time I heard about Marcelo's walk, I was visiting my daughter in New South Wales. Circumstances meant I had to return to Melbourne before I could join him for the last stage of his walk. I was now in contact with him via Facebook and SMS and we arranged to meet in Tarago. Tarago is in rural New South Wales and two days' walk from Canberra. Before leaving, I had to borrow a backpack and put together the rudimentary bits and pieces necessary for undertaking long hikes. On 30 September I caught the early morning bus from Southern Cross Station in Melbourne's CBD to Canberra. I then moved from Canberra by train to the remote town of Tarago. Marcelo met me at the train station. That night we stayed at the Loaded Dog pub. As well as Marcelo, a young Palestinian named Tareq Halawa was present. Over dinner we quickly became pals based on our mutual concern for Palestinian human rights.

We woke early the next morning and made ready for the day ahead after a self-serve breakfast. I will never forget watching Marcelo prepare his severely damaged feet. It entailed quite a procedure of applying bandages, cushioning aids, ointments and strapping. I will also never forget his response when I offered some words of sympathy. He said, 'John, the real suffering is what the Palestinians endure.' By now, Marcelo had covered eight of the ten days between Sydney and Canberra. He was well aware of the requirements of food and water. On that day there were no towns that we would pass through, so food and water had to be carried. Once on the road, Marcelo told me his life story. He was Jewish and born in Argentina, and his family migrated to Israel in 1972. His parents went back to Argentina (horrified by the 1973 Yom Kippur War). In 1983 the Svirskys migrated to Israel once more. Marcelo spent the compulsory time in the Israeli army, but somewhere along the way he had a 'road to Damascus' experience. He could no longer go along with the oppressive policies shown towards the Palestinians. He explained to me that his stand made him unpopular with many of his family and friends.

At least that wasn't something I had to contend with. Most of my Anglo-Saxon family were firmly in the 'not that interested' category. They certainly did not criticise me, nor ostracise me, the way that some members of Marcelo's family had done. Tareq Halawa was born in Jordan like so many Palestinian refugees and displaced persons following the forced expulsions of 1948. He was a friendly and smart young man working in the IT industry in Sydney.

Whilst we walked that morning, Marcelo received an interview of sorts with an Australian Jewish newspaper via mobile phone. Naturally, the newspaper did not agree with his point of view but at least they spoke with him. I'm not sure if the interview ever made it to print. As Marcelo explained, the purpose of activism is to draw attention to an injustice. Therefore, media exposure was desirable. The specific plank of Marcelo's campaign was to call for Boycott, Divestment and Sanctions (BSD) on Israel. I was the oldest of the three of us walking that day and could well remember the boycott campaign to isolate South Africa via similar tactics in the 1970s and 1980s. In South Africa it proved a successful strategy.

The weather was fine and walking was not difficult for me. However, Tareq and I kept an eye on Marcelo who was in a little discomfort, though he never complained. The journey from Tarago to Bungendore took about eight hours. We were famished and enjoyed a large meal of fried food upon arriving in Bungendore. You don't worry about a healthy diet so much whilst undertaking such rigorous physical activity! Tareq made his way off to the Bungendore Railway Station that evening. He had to work in Sydney the next day. All up, Tareq must have accompanied Marcelo for six of the ten days. Marcelo and I stayed the night at the Carrington Motor Inn. After a long day of walking, any bed is welcome, but this place was downright comfortable. I didn't know it at the time, but it was not the last time they would host me overnight.

We had a very early start on 2 October, out walking by 5 am. It was freezing cold so we put pairs of socks on our hands instead of gloves. Marcelo carried a big 'Moses' staff as he trudged along. I could sense some excitement in him, with this being the final day of the walk. In his backpack was a petition which he would present to the Clerk of Petitions upon arrival at Parliament House in Canberra.

We stopped at Queanbeyan for coffee at noon. By this stage my legs were starting to feel quite sore. About three kilometres out of Canberra we were joined by Paul Duffill (Peace and Conflict Studies, University of Sydney) and by Professor Stuart Rees AM, a well-known and highly respected academic (and founder of the Sydney Peace Foundation). Also accompanying us was Shamikh Badra. There was also a small group of wellwishers at Parliament House where we assembled on the front lawns. Marcelo went alone inside Parliament to see the Clerk of Petitions and hand over the signatures. His work was done. By prior arrangement, the Christian Brothers at Daramalan College provided overnight accommodation for us both. Brother John Walker took wonderful care of us in the most noble of Christian traditions.

The next morning Brother John Walker volunteered to drive Marcelo back to Wollongong. John Walker himself is a strong believer in the Palestinian cause. I was almost sad to say goodbye to my new friend Marcelo even though we had known each other just three days. One couldn't help but admire him. He had spent most of his life in Israel and knew the issue inside out. Like all Israelis he had spent some years in the Israel Defense Forces. Yet here he was, actively engaged in the struggle for Palestinian justice. I asked myself this question: How many Iraqis spoke out against the invasion of Kuwait in 1991? How many Indonesians raised their voice when East Timor was invaded in 1975? How many Japanese opposed the invasion of Korea, China and most of South East Asia in the 1940s? History shows that most of us are happy to go along with the side that is winning. Or with the side that looks like it's winning. That is what we are experiencing now. Israel is winning so jump on board. Or at least keep quiet. Marcelo was different. He has the courage of his convictions. And a very sharp intellect too.

After the visit to Parliament House, I had a few hours to wait until the Greyhound bWus transported me back to Melbourne. I wandered the downtown streets of Canberra. No doubt about it, I was hobbling. Walking 68 kilometres was not as easy as I thought it would be. I knew that I had been on a long walk. When I arrived in Melbourne, my wife picked me up from the station and soon enough I resumed my daily life.

The Impact of Marcelo's Walk

IN THE DAYS FOLLOWING, I DECIDED TO SUBMIT AN ARTICLE about Marcelo's walk for the online publication *Mondoweiss*. I asked Marcelo to forward some photos from the walk. The article is as seen below.

MONDOWEISS   *News & Opinion About Palestine, Israel & the United States*

Report from Marcelo Svirsky's epic walk for Palestine

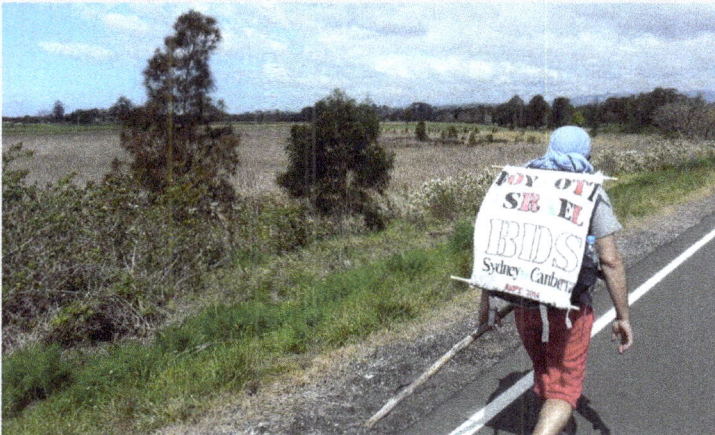

Dr. Marcelo Svirsky

Late last week I joined Dr. Marcelo Svirsky for the last 2 days of his epic walk from Sydney to Canberra. He covered the distance of 287 kilometers (just over 178 miles) in 10 days. The purpose of the walk was to garner support for a petition to present to our Federal Parliament. That petition seeks to promote discussion around the issue of Boycott, Divestment and Sanctions to be levied against Israel.

However, just seeking to promote discussion is an ambitious goal. Australian politicians, overwhelmingly, have been cowered into a situation where any criticism of Israel is problematic!

Marcelo is a Jewish-Israeli academic who continues that strong progressive Jewish tradition of advocacy and activism. As I pounded the pavement with him he spoke at length of his disappointment with the way Israel has evolved into a militaristic state. He left Israel 6 years ago and now has taken up an academic position at the University of Wollongong and we are lucky to have him. He inspires as well as educates. His life's experiences have convinced him that ending the suffering of Palestinians is a cause worth fighting for. His feet were blistered and sore but his spirits high as he marched up that Canberra hill and presented the petition to the Clerk of Petitions. The petition will be read in Parliament on October 27th.

As in America, so in Australia. It is time to give John Kerry a rest. Diplomacy hasn't worked. A grass roots effort to force Israel to start behaving itself seems like the way forward.

John Salisbury

No Australian Members of Parliament or Senators were there in Canberra on 2 October to show support for Marcelo. He had covered plenty of kilometres to try and draw attention to the Palestinian issue. He had also contacted many politicians and media outlets. He was very pleased to read the story about his endeavours in *Mondoweiss*. Then, late in October, he got word that his petition would be spoken of in Parliament. Although Boycotts, Sanctions and Divestments are often used in international relations as a means of bringing rogue states to order, Israel was exempt. For example, Israel itself has always insisted on crippling sanctions against Iran for even contemplating the use of nuclear technology for either civilian or military purposes. North Korea has also had sanctions applied to it. However, no such actions have ever been applied to Israel in spite of their well-known possession of many atomic weapons.

The petition brought to Canberra by Marcelo was asking the Speaker and Members of Parliament to impose BDS on Israel. The petition specifically spoke of the occupation of the West Bank and the siege imposed by Israel on Gaza. Due to the potential power of a boycott against Israel, the pro-Israel forces have opposed it as though their life depended on it. Therefore, it was especially significant that an MP would speak in favour of such a petition.

On 27 October 2014, Melissa Parke (ALP, Member for Freemantle) did just that. Marcelo was elated. He was convinced that she was the first elected official to do so in the Anglophone world. It was wonderful to hear her eloquent, powerful words that night. The next day, as a reaction to her speech, I did something I thought I would never do. I sent flowers to a Member of Parliament. I rang a Canberra florist and arranged for a bouquet to be sent to Ms Parke's office. I later learnt that this MP has an impressive pedigree. She was born in rural Western Australia and has a Master of Laws in public and international law from Murdoch University. She spent a number of years as a lawyer for the United Nations in trouble spots like Kosovo and Lebanon. From 2002 to 2004 she worked in Gaza for the United Nations Relief and Works Agency (UNRWA). Ms Parke's first-hand experiences there appeared to have influenced her. She had a heart as well as a brain.

Melissa Parke's principled speech deserved a wide audience. Those of us who champion the Palestinian cause are a diverse group and from many different parts of the world. They would be pleased and encouraged to hear of her act of solidarity. I decided to write another article and send it to *Mondoweiss*. It was published on 12 November and is included overleaf.

MONDOWEISS
News & Opinion About Palestine, Israel & the United States

Bouquets for Melissa Parke

Earlier this month I wrote an article for Mondoweiss on the story of Jewish-Israeli academic Dr Marcelo Svirsky and his 300 km walk from Sydney to Canberra. The purpose of his walk was to gather support for a BDS Petition against Israel.

The petition was presented to the Australian Parliament and tabled on Monday night. The next day I did something I have never done before: I sent flowers to an elected representative of Parliament. The recipient was Melissa Parke (ALP, Freemantle WA). Parke spoke to the petition on Monday. She was brave and principled. I wanted to show my gratitude to her, and thus the flowers.

Speaking to the petition Parke implored the Parliament to find a solution to end the state-sanctioned violence many Palestinians are currently suffering. She said, '... we know that violence is not the solution. We affirm that the rockets fired from Gaza into Israel are an illegal response to Israel's actions. But it does beg the question: what then is the alternative to the vicious cycle of bloodshed we have witnessed in recent months?'

Suggesting the BDS as a way forward Parke continued, '... nonviolent means of protest are and must be seen as legitimate. It is notable that both Israel and the US approve of boycotts and sanctions against other such states such as Iran and Brunei, so why is it objectionable to boycott a state that is, among other things, committing repeated grave violations of the Fourth Geneva Convention as Israel does with its illegal settlements?'

Echoing the frustration felt by many Parke also said, 'If we are genuinely concerned about national and global security as well as international justice, we, along with other nations, including the US, should be insisting that Israel do its part to lay the groundwork for peace by, among other things, ending its illegal occupation, settlement construction and the Gaza blockade. Until this happens BDS is a perfectly acceptable form of protest and I congratulate Dr Marcelo Svirsky for his courageous walk and his brave stand.'

Although her speech was a *cri de coeur* for common sense and common decency it was remarkable for its uniqueness. No Australian politician, except Parke, would deign to speak up for Palestinian suffering in Parliament. In Australia, as in the US, most politicians are just ventriloquist dolls for the pro-Israel lobby. The same old dross is spouted. For example, 'Israel has the right to defend itself' or 'the bonds between Israel and (insert country here) are unbreakable'. But Monday night Parke walked into no man's land. The brickbats will inevitably follow as our Australian versions of Haim Saban and Jeffrey Goldberg try to take her down. But Melissa, you don't deserve the brickbats, you deserve bouquets. You are, to my knowledge, the first elected representative in an Anglophone country to speak up for a peaceful way to get Israel to start behaving itself. Thank you.

John Salisbury

By now I had become acquainted with Associate Professor Peter Slezak (UNSW). Like Antony Loewenstein, he was a voice of decency and reason from the Australian Jewish community. He advised me that Western Australian Senator Glenn Sterle (ALP) had made a speech in the Senate attacking and denigrating Melissa for her support of the Palestinian cause. His speech was full of Islamophobia and ended with the oh-so familiar line that peace will only come about as a result of negotiations between the two parties. That was becoming a veritable mantra amongst pro-Israel groups, and even those who had little interest in the issue. It was that mantra, plus the line about believing in a two-state solution. As though it was a unique perspective! Those were the two phrases that were such sweet music to Israeli ears. A little research revealed that Senator Serle was a former union official who had been on a number of all expenses paid trips to Israel organised by the Australian pro-Israel lobby AIJAC (Australia/Israel & Jewish Affairs Council). From what I have heard, these trips often result in the participants, thereafter, having an uber-love for Israel. Those attending don't get to see the nasty side of the 50-year occupation of the West Bank. It was depressingly familiar – the indoctrination of our political class by the well-resourced and well-organised Jewish/Israeli organisations. Conversely, those politicians who spoke out against the occupation and the blockade of Gaza were made to feel uncomfortable. And so it was essential to acknowledge their stand.

A Foreign Minister's Epiphany

On 8 November, Bob Carr, one of Australia's former Foreign Ministers in the Gillard government, wrote a piece for *The Australian* newspaper entitled, 'Why I'm Now a Friend of Palestine Rather Than Israel.' In it Mr Carr wrote of his change of heart with that most controversial of countries. His epiphany had real gravitas considering the fact that in 1977 he and ACTU President Bob Hawke (Prime Minister from 1983 to 1991) founded a Labor Friends of Israel group. He wrote of the 47-year-long occupation and the disastrous future for Israel if it continued settlement expansion. Of particular moment was the dramatic increase in settlements, up from 25,000 in 1977 to 500,000 in 2014. 'Settlers won't move. The Israeli government won't force them. So an indefinite occupation morphs into the extremists' goal of a Greater Israel.' Although Mr Carr did not mention it, I am sure he knew that actually the Israeli government sponsor and subsidise settlements. It is the Israeli government itself that builds the roads and provides the infrastructure to enable the settlements to thrive. If you are struggling to buy a home in the pre-1967 Israel, or if you want to immigrate to Israel from Brooklyn or Caulfield but you are not wealthy, then a house in one of the West Bank settlements may be an attractive financial proposition.

Mr Carr continued, 'We have politely pitched the case for Palestinian statehood as creating security for Israel. But in view of the settlements and settler violence, I now pitch the case in terms of the rights of Palestinian people, recognised in international law and every draft peace statement supported by the world for a quarter of a century.'

In his book, *Diary of a Foreign Minister*, released in the same year (2014), he tells of Prime Minister Gillard not even letting him criticise West Bank settlements due to her fear that it would anger Australia's pro-Israel lobby – a reference to the Melbourne-based Australia Israel Jewish Affairs Council (AIJAC) – which Mr Carr said had a direct line into the Prime Minister's office. It certainly confirmed why she would not deign me with a response to my numerous emails and letters. I couldn't help but be surprised that someone on the progressive side of politics would be so forgiving of such a controversial country.

By now the routine pillorying of anybody who dared to speak up for the Palestinian cause was well established. Australia's former Foreign Minister got his fair share. Firstly, from the self-described 'falafel faction' of the Labor Party, Mark Dreyfus and Michael Danby. Mr Carr also received a slamming by Fairfax journalist Peter Hartcher. All three had connections to the lobby. In a wider context, it just meant that not much had changed since Antony Loewenstein put pen to paper in 2006.

I wrote another piece for *Mondoweiss*. It appeared on 11 November 2014 and is printed opposite.

MONDOWEISS   *News & Opinion About Palestine, Israel & the United States*

Sea change down under: Ex–Australian Foreign Minister announces himself a 'Friend of Palestine'

Foreign Minister Bob Carr press conference with US Secretary of State John Kerry on March 18, 2013.

Australia's immediate past Foreign Minister, Bob Carr, has dramatically changed his views with respect to Israel and Palestine. In his article "Why I'm Now a Friend of Palestine" published in last Saturday's *The Weekend Australian* he explains his change of heart:

"Pennant Hills Golf Club in Sydney is an unusual place for an epiphany on the changes in Israel. Still, it was there I met a Christian volunteer who went to the occupied territories to escort Palestinian children to school to protect them from verbal and physical violence by Israeli settlers. Violence against Arab kids? Christian volunteers to protect them? From Jewish settlers? None of this was around in 1977 when I rented a room in Sydney Trades Hall and called on Bob Hawke, ACTU President, to help me launch Labor Friends of Israel. In 1977 the Israeli occupation was 10 years old. There were 25,000 settlers. It was easy to believe the Israelis were holding the West Bank only as a bargaining chip. Arabs were terrorists.

Now the occupation has lasted 47 years. There are now 500,000 settlers. Up to 60 per cent of the Israeli Cabinet is on record as opposing a two-state solution. Palestinians have been part of a peace process for 25 years. Israel has gone from secular to religious. The ultra-Orthodox and religious Zionists hold 30 of the 120 seats in the Knesset. It has gone from cosmopolitan to chauvinist, with some ministers espousing a brand of nationalism like that of France's Le Pen or Austria's Jorg Haider."

Mr. Carr was Premier of New South Wales for 10 years. He was Australia's Foreign Minister up until September 2013, when Labor lost the last federal election. He is an experienced and savvy political figure widely respected by both sides of politics. He is right in the centre of the Australian political firmament. The antithesis of a fringe player. The pro-Israel lobby has gone into overdrive to try and cut him down. Even equating him with David Irving! But Bob Carr carries too much gravitas to dismiss easily. He has strong credentials; he was, after all, the founder of Labor Friends of Israel.

Carr continues:

"Permanent occupation means Israelis get cast as Afrikaners and the world will recognize Palestine and isolate Israel. After all, the alternative would be unthinkable: to accept colonial rule with one religious and racial group enjoying the vote that the majority denied.

We have politely pitched the case for Palestinian statehood as creating security for Israel. But in view of the settlements and settler violence, I now pitch the case in terms of the rights of the Palestinian people, recognised in international law and every draft peace statement supported by the world for a quarter of a century.

Palestinians must commit to non-violent resistance, not a third intifada. They must build international support. They must engage with the righteous Jews who condemn the takeover of Zionism by the fanatics.

Forty years ago I signed up to be president of Labor Friends of Israel; I still count myself a friend of the liberals in that country but it serves the cause of a just peace better by me this week becoming a patron of Labor Friends of Palestine."

It is heartening to see more and more people putting their heads up over the parapet. Mr. Carr is not the first but his standing means something. For the Pro-Israel Lobby to link him with holocaust deniers is laughable and demonstrates the paucity of their argument.

Needless to say, I phoned Mr. Carr's office yesterday to express my appreciation.

John Salisbury

I had by now well and truly left behind my previous misapprehensions about the little country Leon Uris had so convincingly written about in his novel. It felt like there was a growing chorus of people who were disapproving of Israel's behaviour.

In 2014 the ABC broadcast a programme that exposed the awful treatment of Palestinian children by the Israeli army. 'Stone Cold Justice' was a joint report by *Four Corners* and *The Australian* newspaper. For the report, John Lyons won the Walkley Award for investigative journalism. It was a searing account of the blatant discrimination inflicted upon Palestinian children. Once again there was blowback. This time by fellow *The Australian* newspaper journalist Greg Sheridan. He wrote that John Lyons' account was 'evil and untrue'. This, despite the witness of Australian lawyer Gerard Horton, who for many years had been representing Palestinian children detained by the Israeli military. Greg Sheridan was, and is, a huge and constant defender of Israel.

In March of 2015 I met up with Marcelo Svirsky again. He flew down from Wollongong to Melbourne to give a talk on an unrelated matter at Monash University, Clayton. After his presentation we discussed the wash-up from his BDS walk last year and the importance of maintaining momentum. In April he was due to do a presentation at a BDS Conference at Southampton University in England. However, it was cancelled at the last minute as a result of pressure from Israel supporters. So on the battle went, wins and losses.

Another Walk

By the middle of 2015 I had made my mind up. I would do another walk for Palestinian freedom. There would be three aims:

1. Draw attention to the issue of Palestine generally.
2. Reinforce and build upon the momentum of Marcelo's walk of 2014.
3. Present a petition to the Federal Parliament in Canberra.

This time the aim of the walk would centre round recognition of Palestine. I rang the Standing Petitions Committee who advised me on the precise details required in order for the petition to be accepted. They were very helpful and suggested I do a draft and send it to them for approval (only in terms of the format, not the subject matter). I had my petition sorted and began to collect signatures. I had the strong backing of my wife, Wendy, and my daughter, Penelope.

To complete the walk I needed things such as a suitable backpack and the best walking shoes I could find. My daughter set about arranging a calico banner advertising the cause of the walk that I could carry with me. I stocked up on bandages and blister pads, remembering the terrible condition of Marcelo's feet last year.

There was very little help available, via my internet searches, on how to prepare yourself physically for long walks. It was like preparing to run a marathon. I decided that the training programme would be a series of walks of increasing length over several weeks. The first month the training would be three 7-kilometre walks per week. The second month the training would be two 7-kilometre walks, two 14-kilometre walks, one 20-kilometre walk per week. The third month the training would be two 7-kilometre walks, three 15-kilometre walks and one 35-kilometre walk per week. Whilst undertaking these walks, one needs to fill one's backpack with the equivalent weight of books as equal to carrying provisions for the actual walk. Naturally, I got lots of blisters and my legs were a little tender, but by the end of the second month I felt reasonably comfortable. I booked accommodation for each night of the upcoming journey and started a Facebook page entitled Recognise Palestine Walk 2015.

I contacted everyone who I thought may be able to assist with the project. I was put in touch with Jessica Morrison, Executive Officer of APAN (Australian Palestinian Advocacy Network). We met for coffee in the city. She opened up a lot of contacts for me and gave advice on where any support may come from among MPs and Senators. Jessica also pointed me in the direction of Hilmi Appa and Issa Shawesh from the Sydney based APPA (Australian Palestinian Professionals Association). They were ready to support me in Sydney.

Guided by Antony Loewenstein, my daughter and I prepared a press release. Antony was by now a veteran on this issue and had useful things to suggest about what might work for a media release. I rang *The Leader*, our local newspaper. They sent a photographer to our house and published a small article about my intention to walk in support of Palestinian human rights as seen below.

MALVERN EAST

John prepares for trek to Canberra

MALVERN East resident John Salisbury is set to embark on a mammoth 10-day trek from Sydney to Canberra next month.

The 61-year-old retiree (pictured) will walk from the Opera House in Sydney to Canberra's Parliament House to deliver a petition that asks the Federal Government to recognise the state of Palestine.

"My walk is designed to keep the momentum going on this," Mr Salisbury said.

"The Government in Can-

berra don't accept electronic petitions. They only accept hard copy.

"It's quite a physical challenge. It's going to cost me quite a bit of money too.

"I want to get to Parlia-

ment when they're sitting and present the petition to one of our elected representatives."

Mr Salisbury will be accompanied part of the way by friends and family, but expects he will be the only person within his group to walk the entire distance.

"I've got a little program to prepare, the same way you have to prepare for a marathon."

To contact Mr Salisbury, email jtlsalisbury@hotmail.com

As anyone who has collected signatures for a petition can attest, it's not easy. Once you have contacted all family, friends, associates and acquaintances, you only end up with a few hundred signatures. I am advised that doing petitions on social media is considerably easier. However, a petition to the Federal Parliament is only acceptable in pen and paper format. Sometimes signatures came easily, but in my experience, at other times one had to spend a few minutes discussing the issue before someone would put their name to paper. My wife was an absolute champion in this regard and worked very hard. Once I had made my decision to advocate for Palestine, she got on board. Nobody did more than her to make things happen.

It was decided we should do a public signature gathering exercise in our local shopping strip on a Saturday morning shortly before departure day. Our local council advised that such activity required a permit, along with public liability indemnity insurance. We set up our little stall and for three hours engaged passers-by, asking them to sign our petition. It was quite informative as to the level of public support for the long-suffering Palestinians. The majority actually did sign, I'd guess about 60%. Some made comments along the lines that they 'thought the Palestinians had suffered too much', others were 'too busy' or they advised that they 'never sign petitions'. Some people refused to sign because they were strong supporters of Israel, but not many. One surprise to us was the number of people who were quite well informed on the issue. Many were enthusiastic to sign because they considered that the Palestinians had been given a raw deal for far too long.

In 2014, Dr Svirsky struggled to get support for his BDS Petition in Canberra. The 2015 petition was simply asking for Palestinian recognition. Surely it would be easier to gain traction. Emails were sent to some MPs who I was informed were sympathetic to the Palestinian cause. I even rang some of them. Maria Vamvakinou (ALP, Member for Calwell) is Co-Convenor of the Parliamentary Friends of Palestine. She was encouraging of the project and wanted to meet me upon my arrival in Canberra. She asked me to meet her on the day after my arrival as she was to be absent from Canberra on 13 October. Laurie Ferguson (ALP, Member for Werriwa) also gave the project his endorsement and told me he would catch up with me upon my arrival. The wonderful Melissa Parke (ALP, Member for Fremantle) too. These expressions of support encouraged me considerably.

In the meantime, there were quite interesting debates going on within the broader ALP around the Israel/Palestine issue. Former Foreign Minister Bob Carr was the most prominent voice pushing for a more balanced approach to the 70-year-old issue. Even though it appeared hardly controversial that Mr Carr was critical of settlement expansion, he also advocated strongly for recognition of Palestine. The pro-Israel lobby resorted to their tried and true formula of accusing him of anti-Semitism. Could anyone take them seriously? It was laughable and proved the paucity of their arguments.

The Triennial Conference of the ALP was held in Melbourne in July of 2015. A strong argument was put forward for recognition of Palestine. The final wording of the motion was watered down following behind the scenes lobbying by the right-wing faction of the Victorian branch. Rather than simple recognition, the amended wording was 'consult like-minded nations towards recognition of the Palestinian state'. Ultimately, this meant three more years of no action by the ALP whilst Israel built more settlements. Three more years of injustice going unchallenged. However, it was progress in the right direction and pro-Israel lobbyists might be concerned. Manager of Opposition Business in the House Tony Burke spoke to the motion first. He said, 'Australia, under Labor, today makes a commitment that it has to be resolved, and we as a nation, unlike our opponents who argue things like that East Jerusalem is not occupied, we are a party who will speak the truth about the situation.' The motion was seconded by Queensland delegate Wendy Turner who made a stirring speech for Palestinian rights.

In the week before the walk began, I received a telephone call from a reporter for *The Australian* newspaper. After enquiring about the nature and aims of the project, and learning that I had the support of some Parliamentarians, she arranged to send a photographer to my home to take some photographs. It seemed that an article would be printed in the upcoming edition of *The Weekend Australian*. The project was getting some media attention as hoped. Unfortunately, that did not occur. On 2 October, a NSW policeman, Curtis Cheng, was shot and killed by a radicalised Muslim teenager. That story was all across the newspapers on 3 October, leaving no space to write about our walk to highlight the plight of Palestinians.

Day 1 – Sydney Opera House to Sutherland: 4 October 2015

My wife, daughter and stepdaughter all flew into Sydney with me on 3 October. They wished me well and knew I was anxious to get underway. The next morning we taxied to the Opera House. A small group of perhaps 30 supporters, none of whom I had met previously, were there in solidarity. Some of them handed me pages of signatures to add to the petition. It was enormously humbling. By 10 am the walk was underway. Several people walked with me through the CBD and onwards through Redfern and beyond. SBS Radio interviewed me by mobile phone. The weather on 4 October was an unseasonably hot 34 degrees Celsius. Similar temperatures were forecast for the next few days. This walk was not going to be comfortable.

During the first day's walk I came across a group of young Muslim girls and boys 'chilling out' as adolescents of all stripes do. I was conscious of the shooting a couple of days prior in Sydney. They enquired about where I was going and why. I think they were bemused and surprised. I like to think that they got the message that not all Australians of Anglo-Saxon background are prejudiced against Muslims just for being born into that faith. That might have been then Prime Minister Tony Abbott's position, but some of us begged to differ. I hope they never feel marginalised or desperate enough to succumb to radicalisation.

One of the great aspects of being on a project like this is the people you meet. There to wish me well at Sydney Opera House were a great couple, Jim and Diane Dounas. They live in Grays Point which is nearby to Sutherland, the end destination for day one of the walk. They generously picked me up at Sutherland and accommodated me overnight in their home. As it had been such a hot day, I needed to rehydrate copiously. Diane is a committed campaigner for the Palestinian cause. She and her husband feted me that night. I was learning that the cause of the Palestinians had advocates all over the place.

Day 2 – Sutherland to Stanwell Park: 5 October 2015

Diane and Jim Dounas walked with me for a kilometre or two that morning. It was another very hot day. Unlike the previous day, there were virtually no milk bars or service stations where one could rehydrate with a cool drink. At one point I almost collapsed with heat stroke. For a while it felt like I was going to melt into the tarmac. A young couple noticed my condition and stopped their SUV to help me. They gave me mandarins and I gradually recovered enough to keep walking. A long slow struggle to reach Helensburgh and then down to the seaside town of Stanwell Park. I stayed at a bed and breakfast for the night.

Day 3 – Stanwell Park to Dapto: 6 October 2015

Once you leave the large metropolis areas in Australia, you notice a much less cosmopolitan environment. Much less multicultural.

Prior to leaving Melbourne, I rang several NSW Aboriginal Land Councils. I asked their permission to walk on their land. The elders I spoke to appreciated getting my request and granted me permission. A symbolic gesture on my part perhaps, but after all, I am embarking on a walk for human rights.

So it was, as I walked along the beautiful coastline towards Wollongong. I passed through many small towns such as Coledale and Thirroul. Walking over the Sea Cliff Bridge is spectacular and unforgettable. For the third day in a row it was very hot. Once again, I gave the soft drinks a big go. All up, the fitness tracker registered over 50 kilometres that day. I limped into Dapto township and discovered that my pre-booked accommodation was 3 kilometres back towards Wollongong. I was unable to walk another step and so caught a taxi. To add to my discomfort, the taxi driver was very unimpressed with the cause of my venture! Accommodation at the Dandaloo Hotel Motel. Not a flash place but a palace for the footsore, hot and weary traveller. There were many messages of support and encouragement coming through on social media.

Day 4 – Dapto to Robertson: 7 October 2015

The recuperative power of sleep is amazing. My legs had recovered and the weather was much cooler that day. I always remind myself of how fortunate we are in Australia. The Palestinians enjoy no such luck with severe restrictions on where they can go, and when.

The first few kilometres were through a light industrial area to Albion Park. Thereafter, it was a steep ascent through the Macquarie Pass, which is 12 kilometres of narrow, winding road. It was necessary to stand in the ditch as buses and trucks passed by. Even in such difficult terrain I endeavoured to keep in touch with family, friends and supporters. I was also constantly trying to make contact with MPs and Senators, in most cases through their office staff.

At the summit of the pass I put a jacket on. If you are ever in the area, stop off at the famous Robertson Pie Shop. The food there tastes amazing after a long day walking, let me assure you. Three kilometres onwards from the summit pie shop is the delightful Southern Highlands town of Robertson. I stayed at The Robertson Inn. The Recognise Palestine Walk 2015 Facebook page was exploding with love, especially from the global Palestinian community. I also received an SMS from *The Australian* newspaper reporter Jennine Khalik. She advised that an article about the walk was 'not altogether buried'. My spirits were high that night after receiving her call.

Day 5 – Robertson to Moss Vale: 8 October 2015

Word had got around Robertson that somebody had walked through the pass the previous day. Not sure whether they thought me crazy or brave, but once I had explained the reason behind the endeavour, the petition was signed by some townsfolk. I was rapidly learning that most people agreed that if human rights mean anything, they mean that they can't only be applied to people of certain ethnic backgrounds or religions.

The trek from Robertson to Moss Vale was flat for the most part, and only 21 kilometres. It was a relatively easy day in comparison to previous days. There was barely any commercial activity in between but there were plenty of cows to moo me on my way as I trudged by. I was blessed with a cool day again and no aches or pains in my legs. Even the blisters had subsided.

Noel Ferguson of the Southern Highlands Palestine Support Group met me in Moss Vale. The previous year he joined up with Marcelo and he extended the same courtesies to me in 2015. I stayed with him at his house in Mittagong. Noel is a steadfast supporter of the Palestinian cause. That evening, at Noel's house, the Southern Highlands group gathered together for dinner to endorse the project's advocacy for Palestine. There was great company and solidarity. The members had collected some signatures too. Once again, I went to bed very encouraged at the worth of the project.

Day 6 – Moss Vale to Marulan: 9 October 2015

Noel Ferguson has an antiques shop and a residence at the rear of his property. He put his business interests on hold that day and walked with me. What a guy. My appreciation of him was enormous. Using satellite navigation, he had worked out a backroads route to Marulan. Walking on the highway would have been a distance of some 57 kilometres. Across the back roads it was reduced to around 40 kilometres. Noel was terrific company.

We were also joined later in the morning by the Wesley-Smith brothers, Rob and Peter. They are also enthusiastic supporters of the Palestinian struggle. Rob has an interesting story to tell with regards to his strong connections to East Timor. Peter Wesley-Smith was a professor of constitutional law at the University of Hong Kong for many years. Chatting to them along the route and over lunch at the tiny and remote village of Wingello was interesting and satisfying. I learnt from them that Dr Vacy Vlazna had given them my mobile phone number, thus enabling them to contact me. Vacy was there at the Opera House to wish me well on 4 October. She is a fervent and indomitable fighter for the Palestinian cause.

It was another long day's march so the sight of the Marulan Hotel was most welcome. Noel's son was there to drive him back home to Mittagong, whilst I put my feet up for the night. It is hard to describe the level of comfort a humble 'back of Bourke' pub like the Marulan Hotel can provide to a tired and footsore traveller. The hotel only offered a very basic room with a shared shower down the hallway, but it was the equivalent of a palace for me that evening. I consumed a beer or two and some hot food, cooked by a Korean chef who had somehow ended up working in rural New South Wales. It's a wonderful, small world sometimes.

Day 7 – Marulan to Goulburn: 10 October 2015

Waking up in remote Marulan, all one hears is the sound of native birds. I always heard these as a reminder that I must get up and hit the road once more. At the local bakery I purchased a copy of *The Weekend Australian*. There was still no mention of our project. There were no towns along the route that day, so a heavy reliance on dried fruit and nuts was necessary. I quickly discovered why they are the constant trekkers' choice of energy and sustenance. I often found myself thinking how amazing it was that my body was holding up as well as it did. It seemed to be becoming used to the daily rhythm of pounding the pavement.

Most of that day's walk was along the Hume Highway, a flat, boring stretch of concrete that seemed to rise up to meet the horizon forever. A young man stopped his car to offer me a lift. I was, of course, tempted to accept. But, once the purpose of the endeavour is explained to anyone, the temptation of accepting a lift vanishes. However, like quite a few others, the young man signed our petition. After walking 28 kilometres that day, I reached Goulburn, a town of significant size.

I paid only $90 to stay at the Alpine Heritage Motel in Sloane St. It was a Saturday night but not a lot seemed to be going on in the sleepy rural town. For a city boy, it was almost a novelty to be there. One can get food that may no longer even be available in our big cities. The Golden Star Chinese restaurant did a mean combination chow mein, served by Caucasian wait staff! The years just melted away.

The Facebook site surrounding the project was gaining wide support by now. Enormous amounts of love and encouragement were being offered from a wide range of people. The one disappointment with the project so far was the missed opportunity of some publicity in *The Australian* newspaper.

Day 8 – Goulburn to Tarago: 11 October 2015

What a fulfilling and interesting week it had been so far. Each day had been different. Justice for Palestinians was the aim of the project but it had also been almost an adventure too, being out there on the road. Today was a rather tedious day. The distance of 38 kilometres involved passing through no towns or villages. Whereas the first three days were extremely hot, the rest of the journey had given me comfortable temperatures of around 20 degrees Celsius. Tarago was reached in about eight hours. That evening I stayed at the Loaded Dog pub again. It brought back memories of 2014; this was where I first started walking for Palestinian human rights. This was where I met Marcelo and Tareq. As the body was being restored over food and drinks that evening, a message came from the two friends to say that they would join me on the final day's march into Canberra. Also, that day I heard that there were fresh outbreaks of violence in the West Bank and Gaza. It was a further manifestation of the urgency for our elected representatives to formally recognise the State of Palestine.

Day 9 – Tarago to Bungendore: 12 October 2015

At the Loaded Dog pub, the overnight tariff was $40 including breakfast, which you make for yourself in the hotel's kitchen. I was on the road at 7 am after checking the Recognise Palestine Walk 2015 Facebook page. I was making daily reports and posting photographs to keep friends and supporters informed of my progress. It amazes me, the messages of support from faraway places: South Africa, Ireland, Malaysia, Canada, USA. It seemed there were friends everywhere, but Palestine needed them!

All the training done prior to departure had paid dividends in spades. Those 32-kilometre walks in Melbourne had prepared the body magically. Follow-up calls to the emails sent to MPs and Senators who have concern for the welfare of Palestinians were made. Both the House of Representatives and Senate were sitting at the time. I have no doubt elected representatives receive a lot of emails and correspondence and are busy with electoral matters as well as being on various committees etc. I discovered that a phone call usually works better than an email. As much support from them as is possible is positive. Along with delivering the petition, which would no doubt end up on the desk of Foreign Minister Julie Bishop.

Accommodation in Bungendore was once again at the Carrington Motor Inn. I had dinner that evening at the Lake George Hotel. Much to my joy, I also received a telephone call from *The Australian* newspaper reporter Jennine Khalik. She advised that there would be an article on the walk in the next day's paper. That was the best news I had received in a long while. Many of the modest aims of the project were being realised. I was really looking forward to the final day of the walk the next day and the arrival at Parliament House, Canberra.

Day 10 – Bungendore to Canberra: 13 October 2015

This day had an earlier start than usual because the end of the walk needed to coincide with the end of Question Time at 4 pm. Marcelo and Tareq had driven to Bungendore from Sydney and met me at the Carrington at 6 am. The previous year's trio were reunited for the same cause. We made good progress out of Bungendore as the darkness gave way to the sunrise. Each step away from Bungendore felt like a step out of the darkness and into the light. It was as though we could all see the recognition of Palestine on the horizon and we were walking towards it. All of us were in good spirits. We knew full well that freedom for the Palestinians was a long way off, but at least we were not sitting on our hands. I think Marcelo was especially pleased because this year's walk was a strong vindication of his solo effort last year. Every day of this walk could be thought of as a joint effort, as support comes from so many inspirational sources. Not just family and friends but from people I had never met. We were united by one thing: our determination to reach out to Palestinians in solidarity, as they struggle for their freedom.

After three hours of walking we came to a sign indicating we had left New South Wales and were now in the Australian Capital Territory. We stopped in Queanbeyan for coffee. Three times during the day we were engaged by Federal Police. They were curious to know the nature of our activities. I would say they were respectful, perhaps even supportive, once the nature of our activism was explained.

In the final march down the wide boulevards of Canberra, we were met by APAN President Bishop George Browning, and APAN Patron Retired Major General Ian Gordon AO. It felt wonderful when I finally took off the backpack for good on the lawns in front of Parliament House. First up, I was welcomed by Craig Laundy (Liberal, Member for Reid, NSW). He was a most warm and engaging man, who seemed to be heading for a bright future in politics. He was very conscious of the issue of Palestinian dispossession. Shortly thereafter, in the foyer, the remarkable Melissa Parke (ALP, Member for Freemantle, WA) welcomed me, as did Adam Bandt (Greens, Member for Melbourne). Politicians are busy people and they come down to show support as time permits. Two other long-term supporters of the Palestinian cause, Laurie Ferguson (ALP, Member for Werriwa, NSW) and the inimitable Senator Lee Rhiannon (Greens, NSW) also arrived. APAN photographer Judith Deland was also there, taking lots of photographs. Marcelo was pleased that we had built on what he started the previous year. Members of Canberra's Palestinian community were also there to thank me for the activism and advocacy.

On top of all this, the article in *The Australian* that day gladdened the heart. The article was headlined, 'Palestine: the Cause of Our Time.' Drawing attention to Palestinian suffering via Israeli occupation was what the project had been aiming for.

Palestine the cause of our time: trekker

EXCLUSIVE

JENNINE KHALIK

After a 10-day trek, retired restaurateur John Salisbury arrives in Canberra this morning to present a petition to parliamentarians calling on Australia to recognise Palestine.

The Melbourne man who is neither Palestinian nor Israeli, began his 300km hike from the Sydney Opera House. His campaign is endorsed by Richard Di Natale, Adam Bandt and Scott Ludlam of the Greens, as well as Labor's Maria Vamvakinou, Laurie Ferguson and Melissa Parke.

The walk comes at a time when escalating unrest in East Jerusalem and the West Bank has sparked fears of a full-scale Palestinian uprising. The unrest follows the more optimistic and symbolic gesture of the historic raising of the Palestinian flag at the UN in New York last month.

Mr Salisbury, who passed through Bungadore en route to Canberra, called the movement to end Israel's occupation of the Palestinian territories "the cause of our time". "In the past 12 months, France, Sweden and the Vatican have joined the international community recognising Palestine," he said.

In 2012, the UN General Assembly upgraded Palestine's status from "entity" to "state", a change supported by 138

John Salisbury

countries, although Australia abstained from voting.

"Australia's position is embarrassing, deeply embarrassing, and we shouldn't be complicit on the peripheral to expropriating land based on religious entitlement," Mr Salisbury said.

His walk traces the footsteps of Marcelo Svirsky, an Israeli-Australian academic and advocate for boycott, divestments and sanctions against Israel, who walked the route last year in support of Palestinian self-determination.

Endorsing Mr Salisbury's journey, Ms Vamvakinou said Australians generally supported Palestine, and the political world needed to be in step.

Last year, the Australian Palestine Advocacy Network, in conjunction with Ray Morgan Research, found 57 per cent of Australian respondents thought Australia should vote yes in the UN to recognising Palestine. Eight per cent thought Australia should vote against.

WORLD P9

As arranged previously, we had to keep hold of the pages and pages of our petition overnight. I had been asked to return to Parliament House the next day to hand them over to Maria Vamvakinou (ALP, Member for Calwell, VIC).

Among others meeting me on the lawns of Parliament House was Brother John Walker. Like last year, John kindly hosted me overnight at Daramalan College. The hospitality, food, wine and general *bonhomie* of John and other Brothers Paul, David and Harold endeared one to them greatly. Sleep came easily that evening.

Day 11: 14 October 201W5 Canberra

The next morning back at Parliament House, we met Maria Vamvakinou at 10 am in the foyer. Melissa Parke was once again there to show her support. Maria took me upstairs to her office and backgrounded the project ahead of a speech she intended to make in the House about the Palestinian issue generally. She accepted the petition and told us that she will submit it to the Standing Committee on Petitions on our behalf.

As I was leaving Parliament that morning, I made a phone call to the talkback segment of ABC Melbourne radio host Jon Faine. We were granted a couple of minutes to outline the aims of the project on air. It was another opportunity to promote balance when speaking of Israel/Palestine in the broader context. Later that day I boarded a Greyhound bus and I was homeward bound, to Melbourne. The physical part of the project was completed, leaving me physically tired but fulfilled.

On 14 October, Maria Vamvakinou made a lovely speech about the issue in the House of Representatives. Then, on Monday 19 October, Green's Member for Melbourne Adam Bandt made a speech about the Palestinian issue in which he too specifically spoke about the Recognise Palestine Walk 2015. Melissa Parke and Lee Rhiannon also mentioned the project in speeches in the days afterwards.

On the Facebook page we did a wrap-up of the venture, and posted a list of all the people who contributed so much to making the project the success it was. We had not yet achieved the ultimate goal of Recognition but the issue was becoming more mainstream. Another article was written for liberal New York Jewish online publication *Mondoweiss*, entitled 'Antipodean Update'.

MONDOWEISS
News & Opinion About Palestine, Israel & the United States

Antipodean Update

Around this time last year I wrote three articles about the situation in Australia regarding Israel and Palestine. Given recent events, I think it useful to update what has been happening more recently 'Down Under.'

Last year Israeli academic, Dr Marcelo Svirsky, led a protest walk from Sydney to Canberra. The walk was designed to draw attention to the injustice suffered by Palestinians and upon arrival at Parliament House a petition was presented to Federal Parliament asking for a BDS to be implemented against Israel. Last year, I joined Marcelo for the last two days of his walk. All elected representatives shunned our arrival in Canberra, although one MP, Mellissa Parke (ALP Freemantle), subsequently spoke in favour of the petition in the House of Representatives. Shortly afterwards, former Foreign Minister Bob Carr announced he was forming a 'Labor Friends of Palestine' group.

Fast forward 12 months and another three hundred and thirty kilometer walk was embarked upon, this time instigated by me and once again designed to highlight the injustice of Israel's treatment of the Palestinians. I carried with me another petition to Federal Parliament. This year the petition was to ask our elected officials to formally recognise the state of Palestine. This seemed apt because of events that had taken place within the Australian Labor Party.

Whist our current Australian Government retains a very pro-Israel Middle East position (voting against the raising of the Palestinian flag at the UN recently), the opposition Labor Party has been pivoting slightly away from its past unequivocal and unconditional support of Israel. The influence of Bob Carr as a persuasive elder statesman seems to be having an effect. At the July 2015 triennial Labor Party Conference, the issue of Palestinian recognition was hotly debated. Sections of the party proposed a motion that endorsed immediate recognition. Previously dominant pro-Israel factions fought back furiously and managed to water down the final wording of the resolution but the dam was starting to leak. As the Shadow Finance spokesman Tony Burke said, 'It is the case that any Australian Government, in international form, must have a position on these issues. And it is important that when Australia takes those positions it does so in a way that speaks the truth about the situation there.' Tony Burke's speech can be viewed here:

http://youtu.be/eUDx47aYdB8

The Recognise Palestine Walk that I spearheaded this year left the Opera House in Sydney on the 4th October. The project generated significant support. An article on the walk appeared in our national newspaper *The Australian*.

We also managed to garner over 1100 signatures. The Australian Parliament does not, at present, accept cyberspace petitions. So each signature had to be collected by hand, usually after a verbal explanation of the aim of the document.

Upon arriving at Parliament House on the 13th of October we were very pleased to be met by six MPs: Melissa Parke (ALP); Maria Vamvakinou (ALP); Laurie Ferguson (ALP); Craig Laundy (LP); Adam Bandt (Greens); and Lee Rhiannon (Greens).

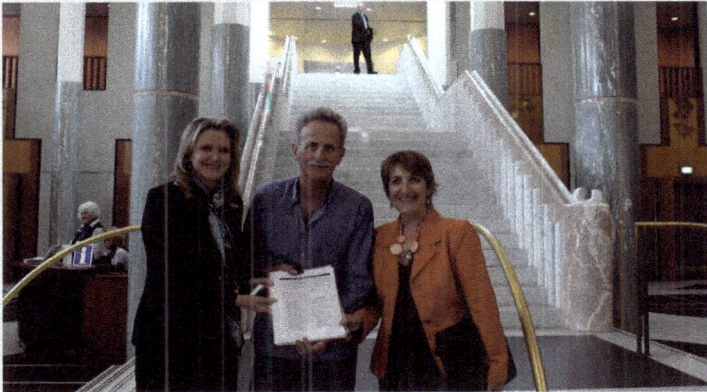

Co-convener of the Parliamentary Friends of Palestine, Maria Vamvakinou MP, was also gracious enough to make a speech in Parliament affirming the aims of the walk on the 15th of October. Her speech can be read here.

Adam Bandt, Greens MP, also made a speech in Parliament referencing the walk that can be viewed here.

For those interested, glimpses of the 2015 protest walk can be viewed on the event's Facebook page: Recognise Palestine Walk 2015.

As a way of drawing attention to the plight of the long-suffering Palestinians the walk proved very effective. It built upon a notable shift in the Labor Party policy. A Morgan Poll in 2014 revealed that 57% of respondents thought Australia should vote 'yes' to Palestinian recognition as an independent Member State of the United Nations. My vox pops experience this year concurs with these figures. We can only hope this momentum is maintained and built upon. Surely the moral and intellectual arguments supporting occupation into the foreseeable future cannot be sustained.

John Salisbury

On 21 October, during a visit to Germany, Israeli PM Netanyahu tried to blame Muslims for the Holocaust. He insinuated Hitler only embarked upon the Holocaust as a result of pressure from the Grand Mufti of Jerusalem, Amin al-Husseini. Chancellor Merkel would not have a bar of it. She insisted that Germans were solely responsible. One wished that Netanyahu and many other Jewish Israelis would be as frank and honest as Merkel and admit their responsibility for the Nakbar (the expulsion of Palestinians from their land in 1948).

On 25 October, my wife and I were invited as guests of honour to APAN's Annual Fundraising Dinner. It was held at Aurora Receptions in Coburg and was a great opportunity to interact with stalwarts of the movement. The MC for the night was Bryan Dawe. Several politicians were there and it was a nice opportunity to be able to thank them personally for the speeches they made in Parliament.

On 7 November, we received a phone call from Hilmi Dabbagh of the Australian Palestinian Professionals Association. They had awarded the project one of three annual awards for Palestinian advocacy. Other recipients that year were journalist Cathy Peters and former Foreign Minister Bob Carr. Unfortunately, we could not fly up to Sydney to receive the award because we had booked an overseas holiday at that time. Marcelo Svirsky agreed to drive down to Sydney from Wollongong and pick up the prize on my behalf.

On 13 November 2015, the Australian Greens, at their National Conference, passed a motion to formally recognise the State of Palestine.

I was the principal signatory to the petition asking the Speaker of the House of Representatives and Members of Parliament to formally recognise the State of Palestine. As such, I was in touch from time to time about the petition. Sharon Bryant was my contact in the office that processes petitions. She eventually advised me that the Standing Committee on Petitions had accepted our petition and had forwarded it to Foreign Minister Julie Bishop. It would now be

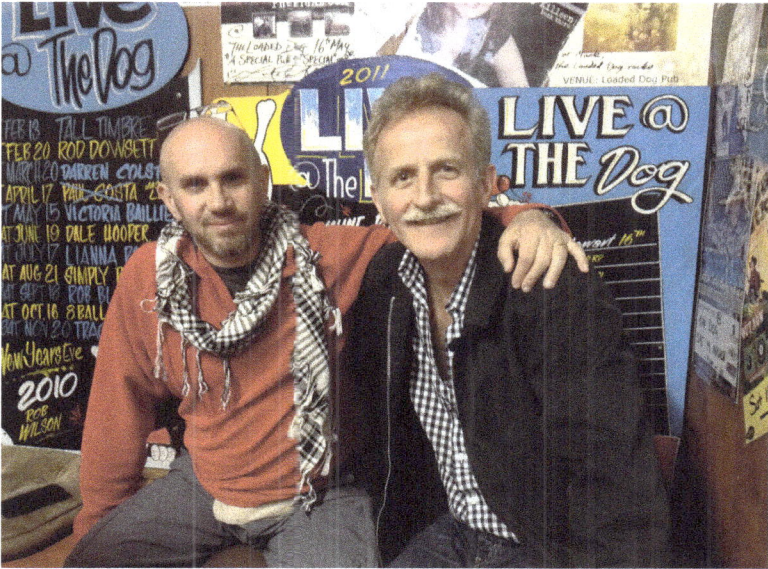

Author and Marcelo Svirsky, October 2014

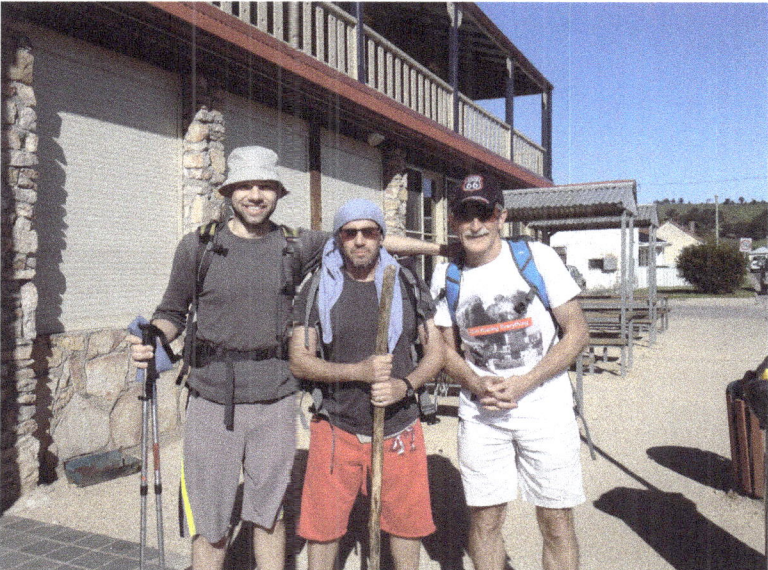

At Tarago with Marcelo and Tareq Halawa

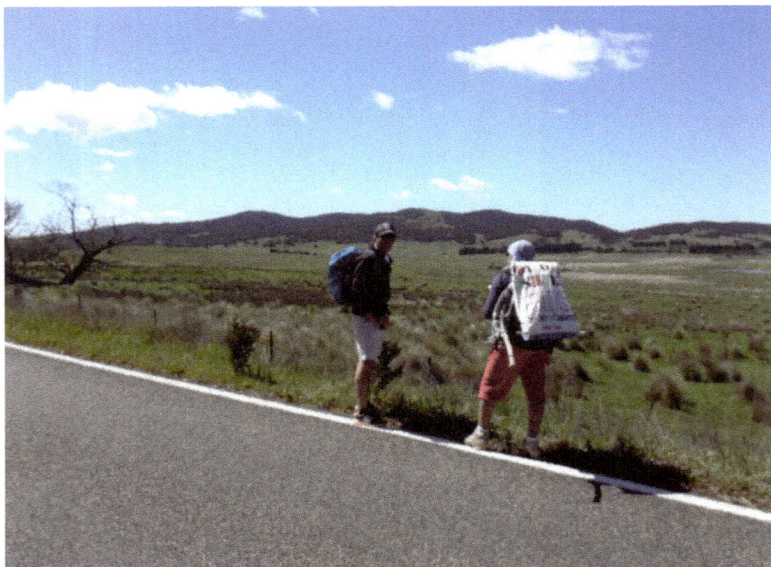

En route to Bungendore, October 2014

Collecting signatures
for the petition,
September 2015

I will miss her

A daughter/supporter

With wellwishers at Sydney Opera House, October 2015

Arrival at Parliament House, October 2015

With Craig Laundy

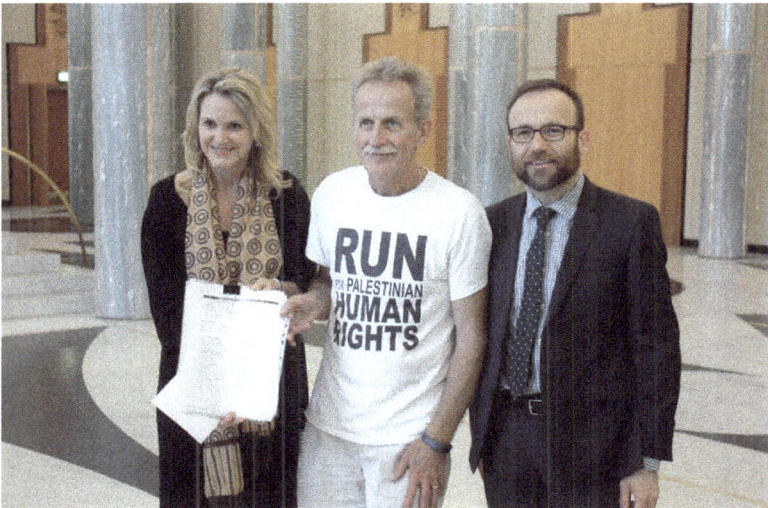

Foyer of Parliament House, with Melissa Parke and Adam Bandt

Collecting signatures once more, September 2016

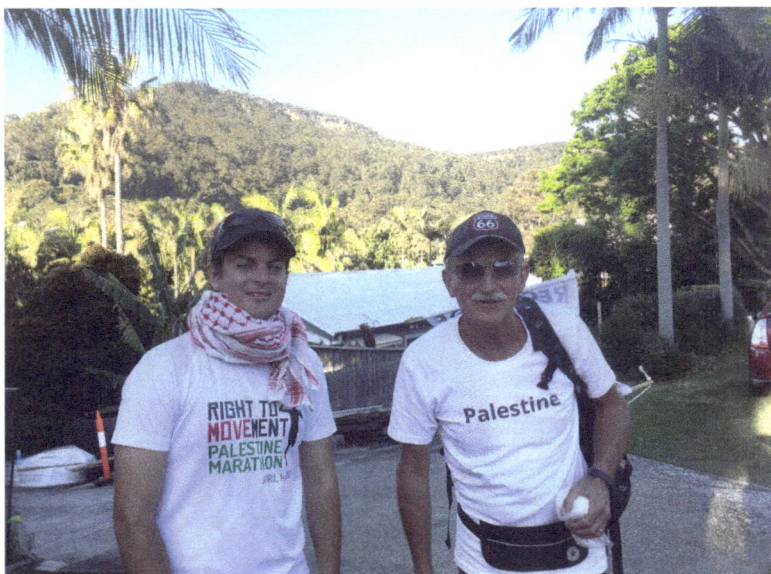

With Patrick Harrison en route from Stanwell Park to Wollongong

Macquarie
Pass about to
be ascended

With Noel
Ferguson in
Moss Vale

Loaded Dog
pub, Tarago.
Reward
after a long
day's walk.

Canberra on the horizon

Parliamentarians and supporters in the foyer of
Parliament House Canberra, , October 2016

1100 - 1597
1100 - 1612

2 1 JAN ...
PETITIONS COMMITTEE

THE HON JULIE BISHOP MP

Minister for Foreign Affairs

Dr Dennis Jensen MP
Chair
House of Representatives Standing Committee on Petitions
Parliament House
CANBERRA   ACT   2600

Dear Mr Jensen

Thank you for your letter of 9 November 2015 regarding the Petition to Formally Recognise a State of Palestine as submitted to the Standing Committee on Petitions for consideration (reference number 1100/1597).

Australia firmly supports a two-state solution to the conflict between Israel and the Palestinians. The Government considers a negotiated two-state solution the only way to establish a future Palestinian state that exists side by side with Israel in peace and security, within internationally recognised borders. Australia has repeatedly encouraged Israel and the Palestinians to return to direct negotiations towards this goal.

Australia remains a committed supporter of the Palestinian people and their aspirations to statehood. We continue to support the institutions of a future Palestinian state through our aid program. In 2015-16 Australia is providing $42.8 million in development assistance to the Palestinian Territories, which includes direct budget support to the Palestinian Authority. This assistance reflects Australia's longstanding commitment to making a practical contribution to the peace process.

I trust this information is of assistance.

Yours sincerely

Julie Bishop

2 1 DEC 2015

her responsibility to respond. I was told that a response to petitions is normally required within 90 days. As we considered Julie Bishop to have a fairly low tolerance level for the Palestinian cause, a quick response was not expected.

To continue to advocate the issue of Palestine, I decided to write a letter to Prime Minister Malcolm Turnbull. Unlike when I wrote to Julia Gillard (several times, by website, and handwritten/envelope delivered) at least he does reply. However, he passed the hot potato on to his Foreign Minister. She did not respond. On two or three occasions I wrote asking for a response directly. No response was forthcoming. It was completely ignored. The petition seemed to be a different matter. On 8 February (just inside the 90-day response time) I received a phone call from the Standing Committee on Petitions advising that they had finally been afforded a response. We got the letter on 16 February 2016. Her tepid and anodyne response is outlined below.

One has to wonder why she thought a two-state solution is the way to go, but only recognised one of the two states? What was she waiting for? She displayed a depressing obeisance and fealty to the Israel lobby. The big end of town that she represented was usually conspicuously absent from any concern about justice in Palestine. Why?

A couple of months later, PM Turnbull called an election for 2 July. There would be an 8-week campaign. APAN (by now I had become a member) had decided to keep the issue of Palestine out there on the hustings. It is undoubtedly true that the situation in the Middle East is not a vote-deciding issue for most people out there in voter land. There are more salient things like tax, health and education that focus electors' minds. That is fair and appropriate. However, the pro-Israel lobby are always advocating that we vote for the party that best supports Israel even if it is not prosecuted in a blatant and partisan way. It is more subtle. APAN asked all MPs and Senators what their views on the Palestinian issue were. For example: recognition of Palestine.

On 13 June, APAN put on an event at Ross House in Flinders Lane, Melbourne. Candidates for the seat of Melbourne were invited to express their views on the Palestinian issue. The Liberal candidate Le Liu did not show up. Both Labor candidate Sophie Ismail and sitting Greens MP Adam Bandt made short presentations. The Labor candidate said that as far as she knew her opponent had only ever made one speech in Parliament about Palestine. That speech must have been the one he made following the walk last October. In a room full of people engaged on this issue, I realised that without our advocacy the Greens MP may not have spoken at all on the topic of Middle East peace. That is not a criticism of the highly regarded Adam Bandt at all. However, that simple fact made an impact on me. The walk had made a difference. After the meeting I spoke briefly to Adam Bandt. He was quite friendly and enquired, 'How are the legs?'

Another Year, Another Walk for Palestine

AROUND THE MIDDLE OF JULY IN 2016, I OPENLY CANVASSED the possibility of undertaking another political walk for Palestine. Whilst my daughter was supportive, my wife was definitely not in favour of it. Every time other options of advocacy were considered, nothing presented itself that would have an impact of the same magnitude. By the end of July, the slow process of training was underway. A new backpack banner was ordered, new runners purchased and topical T-shirts ordered online. Once more a petition was arranged after calling the Standing Committee on Petitions in Canberra. My wife's initial hesitation gave way to her being an industrious collector of signatures. Bless her. APAN said they would once again endorse and promote the project. Fortuitously, many of the board members would be in Canberra on the planned arrival day of 11 October. They were due to host a visit by John Dugard (the former UN Special Rapporteur on Human Rights Commission, Palestinian Territories).

I was assisted by my daughter Penelope to create a new Facebook page. It was immediately embraced by many friends and supporters. On 8 August, a Palestinian solidarity event was put on by the Australian Jewish Democratic Society. The aim of the event, held at the St Kilda beach foreshore, was to highlight Israel's use of water as a tool to dominate and control Palestinians.

Each day a training walk of between 7 and 32 kilometres was undertaken, always with a 7-kilogram backpack on. Whilst walking,

I always carried a page of the petition. Just like last year, we were collecting signatures wherever possible.

Being concerned about the issue of Palestine puts one in good company. There are many examples of this. My older brother Warren had, coincidentally, given me a Henning Mankell novel entitled, *The Troubled Man*. Mankell was the Swedish writer famous for the Kurt Wallander series of crime fiction books which sell in vast numbers. *Wallander* is also an internationally acclaimed TV series starring Kenneth Branagh. What I didn't know, until looking Mankell up on Google, was that he was an outspoken critic of Israel's treatment of the Palestinians. Mankell was on board one of the ships in the Gaza Freedom Flotilla. He pointed out, during a visit to Palestine, that he did not encounter any anti-Semitism, just 'hatred against the occupation that is completely normal and understandable'. He also called for global sanctions against Israel. Mankell died in 2015 at the age of 67. A good man gone too early.

My wife and I had a longstanding Bali holiday booked for September. An interruption to the training schedule was therefore unavoidable. As much as we enjoyed the time away, it was almost a distraction. The freedom walk was front and centre of our minds.

After once more applying for the required permit from City of Stonnington Council, we spent another Saturday morning doing a public appeal for signatures to the petition. Such direct advocacy was both challenging and cathartic, as it was in 2015.

The back problems my wife had been complaining about for the previous couple of months had worsened considerably over the last few days in Bali. She intended to seek immediate medical attention once we got back to Melbourne. In her current state, she would not be able to participate in the Sydney departure arrangements the way she did the previous year.

I ordered another T-shirt from our online supplier that once again promoted the cause we were walking for. We chose to quote from a speech that President Barack Obama made in Cairo in 2009. The lines chosen were:

'Let there be no doubt. The situation for the Palestinians is intolerable.'

Those words were printed on the shirt. Actually, the whole speech was very eloquent in an 'Obamerian' sort of way. What frustrates many of us is that Obama did nothing by way of follow-up. Eight or nine years later, the situation for the Palestinians was still intolerable. The eight years of the Obama presidency promised so much in terms of the Middle East peace process. But nothing was delivered. The only change was a decision to increase aid to Israel by the United States.

By early October my wife was in severe pain with her back problem. So much so that she was bedridden apart from visits to a variety of medical practitioners. I was worried about her and unsure whether the walk should proceed at all. X-rays and MRI scans revealed that my wife had degenerative and bulging discs, with the bulging disc pressing on the sciatic nerve. A toothache in the back seems like some sort of analogy. On 23 September the pain was so severe we had to call an ambulance. Wendy was admitted to The Alfred hospital but they would not operate and only offered strong pain relief. Back problems, it seems, have few easy solutions and neurosurgeons have long waitlists. In desperation we tried a chiropractor who assured us the patient would be 50% better in one week. We decided to proceed with the walk, largely on the basis of his assurance.

Jessica Morrison, the Executive Officer of APAN, gave me a list of the top 20 MPs and Senators who support Palestine. I emailed them, detailing: the aims of the project; the Palestine cause generally; and our request for their support. I have enormous respect for APAN. They really work hard advocating for Palestine. The board members come from Muslim, Jewish, Christian and secular backgrounds. We learnt a lot from them. In many areas they had already travelled the path and knew how to effectively lobby politicians.

Right up until 1 October, I had reservations about going as my wife was still very poorly. It was tough to leave her under such circumstances. Appropriately, it was a very grey day when I made the flight up to Sydney. As she did last year, our daughter Penelope flew down from Byron Bay to meet me in Sydney. The Emerald City was buzzing with activity as it was NRL Grand Final Weekend. We stayed at the very modest Rydges Y Hotel. It was great to hang out with my daughter for the last few hours before the walk began. We went out for a Vietnamese meal. It was not the celebratory night that it had been last year because of Wendy's condition. Penelope tried to bolster my spirits as best as she could. There was never a moment of wavering for the importance of the walk itself.

Recognise Palestine Walk 2016

IN 2016 WE DECIDED TO DEDICATE EACH DAY OF THE WALK IN honour of someone who has made a special contribution to the Palestinian cause or just the cause of human rights generally.

Day 1 – Opera House to Sutherland: 2 October 2016

In honour of Rachel Corrie.

There are not enough words in the English language to express the sorrow and anger one feels over the death of Rachel Corrie. Not only her death is painful, but also the slow and remorseless way the Israeli justice system quashed any attempt to hold anyone accountable for her death.

Rachel Corrie arrived in Palestine from America in 2003. She was unashamedly there as a peace activist. Less than two months after her arrival she was killed by an Israeli armoured bulldozer that was demolishing Palestinian houses. An investigation by the Israeli army concluded that her death was an accident. However, the investigation was criticised by Amnesty International, Human Rights Watch, and several other reputable organisations.

Two subsequent lawsuits, filed by Rachel Corrie's parents, were dismissed. The last dismissal was by the Supreme Court of Israel in 2015. There are many subsequent examples of grotesque behaviour meted out to gentiles by Israel military personnel and the extreme reluctance of the Israeli justice system to adequately punish their own. Please don't mention the names of Moshe Katsav (former Israeli president jailed for rape) or Ehud Olmert (former Israeli prime minister jailed for bribery, fraud and tax evasion). I am referring to punishment for killing, torturing etc. of non-Jewish actors. For example: Elor Azaria (an Israeli soldier who had the misfortune of being videoed whilst executing an incapacitated Palestinian man). He served less than half of an 18-month sentence.

Rachel's parents, Craig and Cindy Corrie, continue her work in support of Palestinian rights through the Rachel Corrie Foundation for Peace and Justice. It is open for a future American president to award her posthumously the Presidential Medal of Freedom, as was awarded to Andrew Goodman and Michael Schwerner. We are always so impressed with the diverse and committed number of people who see the glaring injustice of this issue.

After arriving at Circular Quay, Penelope and I were thrilled to see so many friendly faces, both old (i.e. from the previous year's walk) and new. Those moments with friends and backers would sustain and nourish me on the long lonely roads ahead. I thanked them all from the bottom of my heart, in a brief speech before the 10 am departure. That year about 20 people elected to walk with me through the streets of downtown Sydney as an act of solidarity. Unlike the year before, the temperature was moderate, about 27 degrees Celsius. The 28-kilometre walk was completed by around 4 pm. It was immediately apparent that without training, these long range walks would be so much more difficult, as all around me were ranks of the walking wounded.

Blisters, muscle soreness, assorted cramps etc. aside, we were all united by the common determination to advance the Palestinian cause, and spirits were high. Like the year before, we were hosted for the night by Jim and Diane Dounas at Grays Point. Their house has picturesque views overlooking the Port Hacking Estuary. The Dounas family are some of the world's nicest people. It was a real pleasure and honour to be with them once more. Their home is large, new and extremely comfortable. We were wined and dined like heroes. It was NRL Grand Final night and the victors, the Cronulla

Sharks, were the surrounding suburbs' local team. Cronulla had never won a Grand Final before so celebrations were in full swing throughout the Sutherland Shire. I watched the game's last quarter downstairs in Jim's home theatre. I went to bed still worried by my wife's condition. I had phoned her several times during the day and she assured me she was doing well, but she was fibbing. I wished deeply that things were different. I even contemplated returning home to Melbourne. My enthusiasm for the liberation of Palestine was as strong as ever but home front worries gave me a sleepless night.

Day 2 – Sutherland to Stanwell Park: 3 October 2016
In honour of Hedy Epstein.

For many years we had heard of this marvellous woman and her strong support of the Palestinian cause. Specifically, as an activist associated with Freedom Flotilla boats intending to deliver aid to the blockaded people of Gaza. Hedy was born to a Jewish family in Germany in 1924. She escaped in 1939 and lived most of the rest of her life in America. For many years she spoke out against Israel's military policies. Every year since 2003 she travelled to the West Bank to work with the International Solidarity Movement. She was savagely vilified by many fellow American Jews but honoured by many throughout the world. On that day we walked in remembrance of Hedy's fine work. Hedy died in 2016.

I will forever be indebted to the Dounas family for their hospitality. Diane is a very committed fighter for the Palestinian cause. The next morning they dropped me at Princes Highway after feeding me and making sure I was well prepared for the day ahead. All the excitement of the day before, with a big troop of supporters in tow, had vanished. No company and nothing much to see. Only the relentless whoosh of cars zooming past me. I developed a blister at the 10-kilometre mark but by now I knew how to remedy them effectively. At least the weather was very comfortable, unlike the previous year when heat stroke collapsed me. In 2014 Marcelo chose to go through the Royal National Park, but the asphalt is easier on the feet, so I chose to go on the highway even though it is a few kilometres longer. I had left Grays Point at 9 am. The 27 kilometres was covered in seven hours, stopping at Helensburgh for food. I noticed that there was loads of activity on social media about the walk. It was especially satisfying to learn that many Palestinians in Gaza and the West Bank were conscious of the project. We need to let them know that we see all the pain that they are enduring and that we are doing whatever we can to let them feel they are not forgotten.

Stanwell Park is a small town on the coast popular with holidaymakers from Sydney. My overnight lodgings were at Fernleigh Park Bread and Breakfast again.

Over the past two days we'd had contact with a young man from Wollongong named Patrick Harrison. He would join the walk tomorrow and stay with me all the way to Wollongong. As always, it was heaven to put my feet up at the end of a long day, collect my thoughts, peruse social media, and then sleep.

Day 3 – Stanwell Park to Wollongong: 4 October 2016

In honour of Jo Cox.

In June of 2016, the British Labour Party MP Jo Cox was murdered whilst undertaking constituency work in her West Yorkshire electorate. She was murdered by a 52-year-old right-wing ultra-nationalist named Thomas Alexander Mair. Cox died after being stabbed and shot multiple times. Predictably, her murder was not considered an act of terrorism because her attacker was not a Muslim. As an MP, Jo Cox was noteworthy for her support for ethnic diversity and she championed numerous causes. She was a strong member of Labour Friends of Palestine and the Middle

East. Her calling for the end to the blockade against Gaza was brave and commendable. Prior to entering politics, Jo spent seven years working for Oxfam, an experience that informed her view of international politics. She described the British foreign policy as 'a master class in how not to do foreign policy'. She also bemoaned the lack of what she called 'moral compass' in British policy. She is survived by her husband, Brendon Cox, and their two children. We could do with a lot more politicians who lived with the principles and convictions that Jo Cox had.

Owner of Fernleigh Park Bed and Breakfast, Gail, had baked me a loaf of bread which would sustain me over the long day's march ahead. I received a phone call at 7 am from Patrick Harrison, who was outside and ready to go. He was 'delivered' to Stanwell Park by car thanks to his girlfriend, Jay. This fine young couple, I quickly learnt, had worked in the West Bank. They had seen, personally, the dreadful situation endured by the Palestinians, and were determined to add their voice to those of us expressing outrage.

Patrick had previously joined the Recognise Palestine Walk 2016 Facebook page. He lived in the Wollongong area. His terrific company ensured the project had a great day. Patrick is intelligent, friendly and fit. What could go wrong? The weather was favourable also. The day was full of fantastic coastal vistas as we sauntered along Lawrence Hargrave Drive. It was especially beautiful around the Sea Cliff Bridge area. If you haven't driven along that stretch of coastline in New South Wales, I would highly recommend you put it on your list. The towns of Coalcliff, Clifton, Coledale and Thirroul are most picturesque. We arrived in Wollongong around 2 pm. Marcelo Svirsky lives in Wollongong and had offered to put me up for the night. It was really great to see him, as always. Patrick's partner, Jay, also arrived. They had not only supported the project in person, but also collected a large number of signatures which they passed on to me. Just the best people one could hope to meet.

I was very fortunate to spend a night at the Svirskys. Marcelo is a font of information about what is happening in Israel itself. His parents live there and he visits them frequently. He believes that the push for change must come from outside as Israelis are (in the majority) impervious to considering any meaningful dialogue with the Palestinians. Change, he insists, will not come internally. The only way to get justice for the oppressed is by strong outside pressure being applied to Israel via Boycott, Divestments and Sanctions. Speaking to Marcelo was a reminder of the price some people pay by being Jewish and not blindly supporting Israel. Many of his friends and family have virtually ostracised him for his principled stand. An hour or two with Marcelo was to feel one's batteries being recharged. I must not forget to mention Marcelo's wife, Michal, who runs the City West Cafe in Wollongong. She was very hospitable and kind all the way through my stopover in their city. The previous year I had been alone in a lowly motel in Dapto. What a difference this year.

Day 4 – Wollongong to Robertson: 5 October 2016

In honour of President Jimmy Carter.

No former president of the United States has done more since leaving office to advance global peace than Jimmy Carter. Among the many areas of the world to which he devoted his time and energy was the issue of Israel and Palestine. In 2006 he wrote a book entitled *Palestine: Peace Not Apartheid*. Unsurprisingly, that assessment didn't suit Israel and those that defend Israel. Just like Antony Loewenstein in Australia, President Carter was subject to savage ad hominem attacks. Vicious though they were, the attacks looked pathetic considering his long history of working for solutions to the issue up to and including the Camp David Accords, signed in 1978 between Israel and Egypt.

In November of 2016 President Carter wrote an op-ed article for *The New York Times* in which he implored President Obama 'to grant American diplomatic recognition to the State of Palestine' and to 'do it before his term expires on January 20, 2017'.

It was another perfect day for walking. Marcelo drove me down to Michal's cafe where she cooked some breakfast for us both. Shortly thereafter Marcelo drove me to the beginning point of Day 4, near Dapto. After 10 kilometres of flat terrain, I passed Albion and began the long slog up through Macquarie Pass. I spent quite a lot of the day using the smartphone. I was either ringing MPs and Senators or emailing them. Getting the message through to the actual person can be a torturous process as all of them have minders, assistants, secretaries, chiefs of staff etc. who organise and prioritise politicians' programmes and schedules. I covered the 8 kilometres of steep ascent for a second year without incident. The temperature was fine and physically the body was issue free. In the delightful Southern Highlands town of Robertson, that evening's accommodation was at the Robertson Country Motel. The previous year I had stayed at the Robertson Inn but the upstairs accommodation area was being renovated. Still, just like last year, I had dinner in front of the fire. I met a group of five retirees who engaged me, whilst eating dinner, at an adjacent table. Upon explaining what the project was attempting to achieve, they all agreed to sign our petition.

Day 5 – Robertson to Moss Vale: 6 October 2016

In honour of Ruth First.

A personal favourite for many years has been South African activist Ruth First. She is somebody who deserves to be remembered, even though she was not involved at all with the movement for Palestinian justice. Joe Slovo, her husband, was Housing Minister in Nelson Mandela's 1992 government. Both Ruth and Joe were Jewish. Their opposition to white supremacist policies during the South African apartheid period resulted in their imprisonment and, later, their exile from the country. Ruth eventually ended up living in Mozambique. Ruth was a professor and research director at the Centre for African Studies at Eduardo Mondlane University. In 1982, following a UNESCO conference at the Centre, she was assassinated courtesy of a letter bomb sent by South African Security Services.

All her life Ruth First fought against racism. Inclusive and egalitarian in her orientation, she struggled not for herself but for the disadvantaged, indigenous people of South Africa. Perhaps her Jewish background meant that she had some insight into what discrimination felt like. Though there is no record of her particular involvement with Palestine, she was a close friend of Nelson Mandela, who famously said, 'We know too well that our freedom is incomplete without the freedom of Palestinians.'

I left the small but charming town of Robertson late that morning, after breakfast and chats with locals in a little cafe, where a few more signatures were garnered. My swag was on my back and the loins were girded for another day of pounding the pavement. By this time I was definitely counting down the days until the halfway point was marked. Several telephone calls a day to my wife indicated that her health was not improving. I decided I could not delay my return home once I reached Canberra.

The terrain that day was mostly flat and easy walking. The distance was only a moderate 21.4 kilometres. It was rich grazing land. There were no towns in between so water and snacks were carried, as always. I worked on the list of politicians to contact, as always. Annoying and lobbying might be thought of as synonyms at times. However, I was learning that this was the way business is done. I was trying to be careful not to annoy potential supporters, whilst on the other hand recognising that gathering support was crucial. I was once again liaising with Jessica Morrison who was in Canberra organising the visit of South African jurist John Dugard. She had spoken to former MP Melissa Parke who would be in Canberra and had agreed to meet us on the front lawns of Parliament House on

11 October. Jessica advised me that two supportive Senators (Lisa Singh and Anne Urquhart, both ALP, Tasmania) were unavailable due to overseas study tours. Craig Laundy and Maria Vamvakinou, as earlier indicated, had agreed to be there after Question Time. We needed to build on those numbers.

I felt privileged once again to be met by the sterling Noel Ferguson of the Southern Highlands Palestinian Support Network. Over dinner that evening we discussed the wins and losses of this long political campaign. Both of us were hoping that President Obama would make a gesture towards Palestine in the final months of his presidency. All the hopes and aspirations of the Palestinian people for a true honest broker seemed to have evaporated. Change would have to come from the bottom up. Both Noel and I had lived through the South African apartheid struggle, which looked like an unwinnable battle for many years. I was very fortunate to be hosted overnight again by Noel.

Day 6 – Moss Vale to Marulan: 7 October 2016

In Honour of Daniel Barenboim.

Of all living orchestra conductors, Daniel Barenboim is my favourite. For me he is especially memorable for the 2012 Beethoven Concerts at the Royal Albert Hall. All nine Symphonies of Ludwig van Beethoven were played with Barenboim's inimitable verve and style. All nine are available to watch on YouTube. If, like me, you have been listening to modern music all your life, then Beethoven is a revelation. It is a whole new world of listening pleasure. I have even heard ABC Radio National's Music Show host Andrew Ford say that he gave up believing in God – Beethoven replaced him!

Barenboim was born into a Jewish family that lived in Buenos Aires. When he was ten years old the family moved to Israel. He now lives in Berlin. In 1999, together with the Palestinian academic Edward Said, Barenboim set up the West-Eastern Divan Orchestra.

Musicians who play in this orchestra are drawn from Middle East countries, including Egypt, Iran, Israel, Jordan, Lebanon, Palestine, Syria, and Spain. The aim is to promote understanding between people of different backgrounds through playing music together.

Barenboim has spoken several times in support of the Palestinian cause. For example, he addressed the Israel Knesset in 2004 (The Electronic Intifada, 16 May 2004). He said:

'I am asking today, with deep sorrow: can we, despite all our achievements, ignore the intolerable gap between what the Declaration of Independence promised and what was fulfilled, the gap between the ideas and the reality of Israel? Does the condition of occupation and domination over another people fit the Declaration of Independence? Is there any sense in the independence of one at the expense of the other? Can the Jewish people, whose history is a record of continued suffering and relentless persecution, allow themselves to be indifferent to the rights and suffering of a neighbouring people? Can the state of Israel allow itself an unrealistic dream of an ideological end to the conflict instead of pursuing a pragmatic, humanitarian one based on social justice?'

He has called the occupation of Gaza and the West Bank immoral (danielbarenboim.com, 10 June 2017). Oh that there were more like him – seeing the woods and seeing the trees too.

7 am. Noel and I, having had our large bowl of muesli in the house behind Merchant of Welby Antiques, could be seen making our way to Sutton Forrest from whence the day's journey began. Once again the redoubtable Noel Ferguson was navigating his way via back bush roads towards the day's destination, Marulan. Sometimes the shortcut was heavy going. Just like the previous year we had to negotiate heavy thickets of blackberry bushes and quite a

deep creek. It felt like a boys' own adventure for two men who are past the meridian of life.

There is a forestry industry in this part of New South Wales. A freight-only railroad to transport nature's bounty was a constant part of that day's rural vista. We stopped at Penrose for lunch before Noel was picked up by his son and he returned to the antique shop for the afternoon. I continued, now a solo traveller, along Highland Way to Tallong. The journey was especially long that day. In spite of Noel's shortcuts, the fitness tracker indicated a distance of 46 kilometres covered. A couple of kilometres before Highland Way met the M31 Highway, that familiar car of Noel's appeared. By now feeling weary, I gratefully accepted the lift to the Marulan Hotel. Thank you, Noel. You and I will always share that little bit of solidarity.

It is surprising how much one becomes endeared to a tiny town like Marulan out there in rural New South Wales. If you walk all day, a backpack weighing you down, all you look forward to is food and rest. Despite the modest nature of the Marulan Hotel, it was looked forward to as if it were a palace. I noted the modern nature of Australia once again that year. The chef was the same Korean gentleman as the previous year. Most of the fare was pub standard but a little of the purveyor's background had slipped in on the menu. I spent an enjoyable night at the bar and dining room overhearing the chat of the locals and their families. I couldn't help but think how lucky we are in Australia to live such free and prosperous lives, and how different are the lives of Palestinians. Is it too much to demand that they be able to break free from the yoke of unequal treatment? That is what we were walking for.

Day 7 – Marulan to Goulburn: 8 October 2016

In honour of Roger Waters.

Who would have thought that the legendary bass player from the music group Pink Floyd would become the most principled, most conscience-driven rock musician of our generation? Thirty years ago, if you were to pick music stars with concerns for social justice, 'spoilt for choice' may have been the appropriate cliché. Not now. So many musicians have ignored the call by 140 Palestinian civil society organisations to boycott Israel whilst the illegal occupation of territory persists. Roger Waters stands head and shoulders above his colleagues. He has devoted a lot of time to writing to every artist scheduled to perform in Israel (usually Tel Aviv is part of a European tour package) asking them to consider dropping out and to respect the call from Palestinian civil societies to not play in Israel. Seldom do they heed his entreaties. Renowned Haaretz journalist Gideon Levy says, however, that 'there's no question he has created a new international mood. He feels strongly that the injustice done to the Palestinians must be remedied and he believes he is toiling on behalf of this cause.' To quote Waters himself (in APAN discussion, 1 March 2018, Melbourne), 'In the 1970s and '80s there was no question – we all focused on South Africa because it was the obvious place to focus. It was the place where it looked like all of us who took part in the Anti-Apartheid Movement, as it was called then, might have an effect, and might cause changes in the policy in that small part of the world. Israel is that bit of the world now. Whether Israelis or anyone else likes it or not, it just is.' Sentiments with which all those involved in this project would concur.

It was Saturday morning in Marulan again. Nothing had changed here in rural New South Wales from the year before. I sauntered down the corridor of this outback pub to the communal shower, then off on the road before most of the town had woken up. The weather was mild, perfect, in fact. Just a long, lonely slog along the Hume Highway for 28 kilometres. That day, being Saturday, was not a day to lobby our elected officials, as their offices were mostly closed over the weekend.

There was no such curfew for making calls to my long-suffering wife. As much as I loved calling her, there was an element of guilt that punctuated each contact with her. She was still desperately unwell and needed me to look after her. This was the worst part of this journey, not being there with her.

There were reports in the media about President Barack Obama making a last minute gesture to Middle East peace. On his first day as president on 21 January 2009 he, reputedly, made his first international telephone calls to Egyptian President Hosni Mubarak, Jordan's King Abdullah, Israeli Prime Minister Ehud Olmert, and Palestinian President Mahmoud Abbas. He allegedly said, 'I will deploy every possible effort to achieve peace as quickly as possible.' Nearly eight years later, the most powerful man in the world had come up empty-handed. The 'intolerable situation' he spoke of had only become more intolerable. Settlements across the Green Line had only become more numerous and more entrenched. The siege of Gaza had only become more entrenched. In his last days as leader, would his own frustration boil over and a gesture be made at the UN Security Council or another international forum? Worse still, the likely next president (polls indicated it would almost certainly be Hillary Clinton) was an even more enthusiastic supporter of Israel. How must the long-suffering Palestinians have been feeling?

There were no towns or villages at all on the route that day. Three kilometres outside Goulburn I was pleased to see a fast food restaurant. The weary and famished are not fussy. The large country town of Goulburn was reached by 4 pm. I booked into the Alpine Heritage Motel again. The overnight tariff was $90. It was a modest establishment but was in keeping with the modest aspirations of this project and its chief protagonist. I enjoyed a hot shower and a rest before venturing out to stock up on provisions for the next day. There were just a few days to go before the arrival in Canberra.

Day 8 – Goulburn to Tarago: 9 October 2016
In honour of Henning Mankell.

The Swedish author Mankell has been mentioned earlier in these pages. The late Henning Mankell was one of the most successful of the 'Nordic Noir' group of authors. His writing was tasteful and delved into the character of detective Wallander with great insight into the human condition. Both Swedish and English adaptations made it to our TV screens. Mankell used the, not inconsiderable, wealth from his works to support an array of worthy causes. Many of the charities he donated to were connected to Africa, especially Mozambique. He said, 'There are too many people in the world who just sit and watch their money pile up, that is very hard for me to understand.' Palestine and the cruel injustice perpetrated against them was a chief preoccupation for Mankell. In 2010 he was on board one of the ships in the Gaza Freedom Flotilla that was boarded by Israeli military forces. Eight or nine people were shot. A brave and principled man, Mankell died of cancer in October 2015, at the age of 67.

The distance that needed to be covered on that day was 38 kilometres. I had to leave Goulburn at 7.30 am and walk past the railway yards, slowly leaving civilisation behind. The route taken was along Braidwood Road. There was only the near constant sight of healthy bovine creatures, doing what they do best, to keep me company. For some reason that day I wondered about the whole point of the project – but never for a moment about the cause for which we were fighting. I arrived at the Loaded Dog Hotel at 3.30 pm. I noticed that the pub was for sale. Nonetheless, the publicans, Mark and Nicole, provided a friendly welcoming environment. Being here in October for the third year in a row, they almost knew me. It was $40 per night lodging and breakfast (made by yourself in the pub's kitchen!). You felt the country charm and warmth.

Day 9 – Tarago to Bungendore: 10 October 2016

In honour of Andrew Goodman and Michael Schwerner.

The film *Mississippi Burning* (1988) drew my attention to these two wonderful men. They were social activists from New York and Massachusetts who travelled south to the State of Mississippi in 1964. The purpose of their travel was to assist with voter registrations for African Americans. It was a change sweeping the South as part of the Civil Rights movement. The end of discrimination was well overdue in America but still an anathema to Southern whites. Along with a local African American man, James Chaney, Goodman and Schwerner were murdered by elements of the Ku Klux Klan. The death of these two white men, and the fact that they were from the North, drew attention to the incident and it captured the nation's concerns. Civil rights legislation ending discrimination followed. Despite overwhelming evidence, convicting Klansmen in Mississippi was not easy and only one man served six years in jail. In 2005, the main perpetrator, Edgar Ray Killen, was finally brought to face justice. He was sentenced to 60 years in prison. The death of these two men highlighted the endemic racism of the southern states of America. These men took a stand against racial segregation and, for that stand, they paid with their lives.

In 2014 the families of the two men were presented with the Presidential Medal of Freedom by President Barack Obama. Whilst not involved with the situation of Israel/Palestine itself, their activism to end discrimination is inspiring to those keen to remedy today's discriminations. One can only hope that in years to come Rachel Corrie will similarly be honoured by some future US president.

There was no chance of me buying this iconic pub in rural New South Wales, but these places have a unique character. For small places in remote areas they seem to be the only businesses that can still eke out a living. As such they become almost a rural hub or community centre for locals. For the third year in a row I was up and on the road early and once again there was not a pit stop anywhere from there until Bungendore.

As it was Monday, I began my task of contacting our federal politicians again. I was a little unsure as to how many would come down to say hello at the Parliament House foyer the following day. In a sense, it didn't matter. Most politicians had very busy schedules and duties. The main thing was that I had contacted them and they had heard about the project (they would get much more lobbying and badgering from the Zionist crowd). Jessica Morrison advised today that Adam Bandt was sick and Craig Laundy would be attending a funeral, so those two would not be able to attend. At about the 18-kilometre mark, a passing motorist stopped to say hello. It turned out to be the inimitable Dr Vacy Vlazna who was on her way to Canberra with her own project in solidarity with Palestine. She showered me with drink and foodstuffs. She also offered kind words of encouragement and solidarity.

Towards the end of the day the weather turned decidedly inclement. Five kilometres from Bungendore and the rain and wind were so bad that just making it to town was a relief. The Carrington Inn was palatial at $127 per night, but the extra level of comfort was well appreciated. I had dinner at the Lake George Hotel. I made three calls to my wife who, worryingly, was no better than before I had left Melbourne on 1 October. I heard that Tareq Halawa and Cloighi Ni Fhlannbhra had been out this weekend collecting signatures for our petition with great success. I had an early start the next day so I went to bed early.

Day 10 – From Bungendore to Canberra: 11 October 2016

In honour of Desmond Tutu.

Desmond Tutu was the Anglican Archbishop of Cape Town from 1986 to 1996. As such, he was the most senior cleric in the Anglican Church of South Africa, and the first black African to hold the position. Tutu won the Nobel Peace Prize in 1984 for his efforts in ending apartheid in South Africa. He was an icon for black South Africans during the struggle for freedom, whilst Nelson Mandela was imprisoned on Robben Island. His passport was often confiscated by the Afrikaans government. Following the end of apartheid, he headed up the Truth and Reconciliation Commission. Archbishop Tutu had spoken out against racial discrimination all his life. He had been critical of current South African governments for their inaction on tackling poverty. In 2008 he also called for the Zimbabwe President Robert Mugabe to resign. Tutu had been a strong moral voice across many decades. Importantly, Archbishop Tutu had spoken out against Israel's treatment of the Palestinians – comparing it to treatment of black South Africans under apartheid.

I was up at 4.30 am and away in the dark at 5 am. It was rather cold, so I wore a pair of socks on my hands as gloves. The excitement of finishing was now quite consuming. The road from Bungendore to Canberra was quiet and rural. However, after approximately five hours I gradually climbed to an elevation point where a large sign indicated that I was now entering the Australian Capital Territory. In the distance I began to make out buildings of the nation's capital. The traffic began to build up. I stopped for an early lunch at Queanbeyan. I managed to get through on the Talkback Line to the Jon Faine Programme, 774 ABC Melbourne. I spoke to Raf Epstein who was filling in for Jon Faine. When I explained the reason for our project, he wondered out loud 'if it would be effectual in any way?' In response, I compared the recognition of Palestine by our

Parliament to the enactment of marriage equality by our Parliament. What had been virtually unthinkable only a few short years ago was then almost a reality thanks to the hard work put in by MP Warren Entsch and many others. I said, 'Definitely nothing will happen if we don't get up off the couch and agitate.' There was so much more to say, but getting the issue of Palestine out there in people's consciousness was the most important beginning.

By 3 pm the 40 kilometres had been covered. I had a feeling of relief, together with a feeling of some accomplishment. I am told marathon runners have that same feeling. On the lawns outside Parliament House quite a little crowd had gathered to cheer me on. The wellwishers and supporters are never far away if you are fighting for Palestine. I was especially flattered to be met by former ALP Member for Freemantle, Melissa Clarke. I was handed several more pages of signatures for the petition from supporters, including Tareq Halawa and Kylie Grace. We would end up with between 1700 and 2000 signatures. In 2015 we got somewhere in between 1100 and 1200 signatures. In a sense it may not have mattered. Julie Bishop would probably dismiss the claims for recognition as casually as only someone with a hardened heart could possibly do. Our aim was to keep the issue bubbling along and remind her that it would not easily go away.

Together with APAN board members we moved from the outside grounds to the foyer of Parliament House. The following MPs and Senators came down to meet and greet: Maria Vamvakinou, Gavin Marshall, Josh Wilson, Janet Rice, Anne Aly and Lee Rhiannon. Many others expressed support but could not show up due to parliamentary commitments. The issue of Palestine was being solidly put in front of our elected officials. It always needs to be said that any MPs and Senators who expressed concern for Palestinian human rights were made to feel uncomfortable by the anti-Palestine group who so vigorously prosecute their claim that Israel can do no wrong. Buttressing their stand was a necessity.

Co-Convenor of the Parliamentary Friends of Palestine, Maria Vamvakinou, accepted the petition and told us she would take it to the Standing Committee of Petitions in the next day or two. At the same time as the completion of the walk, APAN was hosting an event in Canberra, with noted South African jurist John Dugard speaking. He spoke at the Press Club that day. The title of his address was 'The US Elections and the Implications for Palestine and Israel, Including Factors Which May Influence the Re-Calibration of Middle East Policies of US Allies, Including Australia.'

I was very fortunate to be among so many friends here in Canberra. Nasser Mashni, the APAN Treasurer, allowed me to use his hotel room to freshen up before a special gathering at Ottoman Restaurant to hear John Dugard speak once more. The dinner was put on by APAN and a great number of our elected representatives showed up. There were about 20 in all, including Senator Doug Cameron and prominent MP Anthony Albanese.

There was a terrific atmosphere and John Dugard's brief address was sharp and concise. APAN President George Browning presented an award for the Recognise Palestine Walk 2016 project. I humbly received it on behalf of all the people involved in the project. It was a night to remember and a huge fillip to the tireless efforts of APAN as they go about their work of fighting for Palestinian human rights. That evening I caught the midnight bus out of Canberra. Upon arriving back in Melbourne the next morning, I immediately drove my wife to a neurosurgeon who began to put back together my wife's back over several weeks.

Reflection and Review

After the Recognise Palestine Walk 2016 was completed, there was the inevitable reflection and review. We definitely seemed to be making progress with the issue of Palestine. The issue was much more prominent than the pro-Israel lobby would wish. On the other hand, there was still a long journey to go. Those hard fought for signatures for our petition would soon be on Julie Bishop's desk. Would she give it even a passing thought? Had anything changed since last year? That year I decided to write to the Prime Minister himself, asking for him to respond rather than pass it on to his Foreign Minister as he did the previous year. The result: no reply.

Is it hopeless, this cause we fight for? Far from it. After all, not replying to letters regarding the issue of Palestine is not the exclusive domain of the conservative wing of Australian politics. Former Prime Minister Julia Gillard was equally unprepared to communicate on the issue. However, just like with the South African apartheid issue of 30 or 40 years ago, it is most likely on the progressive side of politics that change will come.

Whilst our then Foreign Minister Julie Bishop was a dyed-in-the-wool supporter of Israel (she would never deign to criticise that country in the way she scolded New Zealand in late 2017), her predecessor as Foreign Minister was not. These days Bob Carr is very conscious of the perpetual undermining of the two-state solution by settlement building in occupied Palestine. Whilst the Greens have formally moved to include recognition of Palestine as part of their policy platform, they were unlikely to be the party of government in the near future, so it was the Labor Party, leading up to the 2019 Federal Election, that we had to concentrate our activism towards.

As 2016 drew to a close, the world's attention turned to the presidential campaigns of Hillary Clinton and Donald Trump. The former presented a grim prospect for Palestinians, with her long refusal to speak the truth about Israel's egregious behaviour well known. Donald Trump was an unknown quantity, mainly because of his real estate/reality TV star status. The Republican candidate had never held an elected public position before. He said of the Middle East process that fixing it would be 'the deal of the century'. It wasn't much to go on. On 9 November, to the surprise of many, Donald Trump was elected the 45th President of the United States of America.

On 6 November, the annual Run for Palestine event was held in Melbourne. The event was put on by the Australian Friends of Palestine and was an event I had participated in for several years. As well as raising awareness of the Palestinian struggle for freedom and human rights, funds raised go to disabled and orphaned Palestinian children.

Palestinian National Day was held at Federation Square Melbourne on 15 November with great gusto and enthusiasm. The Australian-Palestinian playwright, Samah Sabawi, spoke to the assembled crowd.

APAN continued its advocacy in Canberra with an excellent initiative in late November entitled 'No Way to Treat a Child'. The initiative highlighted the appalling treatment of Palestinian children by Israel. Some 250 children are imprisoned by Israel as I write this. Since 2015, 6000 Palestinian children have been detained. Forty-nine of our elected representatives signed their name to the cause.

On 5 December, US Secretary of State John Kerry was welcomed to the Saban Forum in Washington DC. This is an annual event put on by media mogul Haim Saban. Saban has dual Israeli/USA citizenship. It is worth mentioning the political proclivities of this

Printed with kind permission from Cathy Wilcox

billionaire. He proudly proclaims that he 'is a one issue guy and my issue is Israel'. It was no surprise that Secretary of State John Kerry showed up. Previous guests include Hillary Clinton and Barack Obama. The purpose of the forum is to ensure the USA government always treats Israel favourably (to say the least). When questioned about how Mr Saban pursues his singular issue in politics, his reply was, 'I make donations to political parties, establish think tanks, and control media outlets' (Diana Johnstone, *Queen of Chaos: The Misadventures of Hillary Clinton*).

Also in December 2016, President-Elect Trump announced his appointment of David Friedman as the USA Ambassador to Israel. Mr Friedman distinguished himself, prior to his appointment, by being a no-holds-barred, boots-and-all supporter of Israel. He even headed up a group named the Friends of Bet El Institutions. This is an organisation that advocates against a two-state solution, and even provides $2 million to the Israeli settlement of Bet El. There was not much doubt that he would be an extremely suitable person to represent Israeli interests to America.

It is also worth noting that as of August 2018, Australia, a country that (unlike Israel) has always been in the trenches with America in every conflict since World War II, still did not have an appointed US Ambassador to Australia. Why is Israel a higher priority than Australia in getting a new Ambassador?

President Obama's Parting Gesture

On 23 December, something remarkable happened at the United Nations. Security Council Resolution 2334 was adopted. For the first time in the Obama presidency, the United States abstained, rather than use its veto power, on any UN resolution critical of Israel. Resolution 2334 demands a halt to Israeli settlement activity and said such activity constitutes a 'flagrant violation' of international law.

The draft document of Resolution 2334 was initially presented by Egypt on 22 December. However, under intense pressure from President-Elect Trump, Egypt withdrew the proposal. Unfortunately for Israel, the proposal was then presented to the Security Council again on 23 December. This time the draft was presented by four other members of the Security Council, New Zealand, Senegal, Malaysia and Venezuela. Israel tried in vain to get New Zealand to withdraw, but it was unsuccessful. Bibi Netanyahu told New Zealand Foreign Minister Murray McCully that Israel considered that a 'declaration of war' and recalled its ambassador from New Zealand. Not surprisingly, Israel has not complied with the terms of the resolution. Settlements, though illegal, continue to be built throughout the West Bank. I sent an email to the New Zealand Foreign Minister expressing admiration for New Zealand's presenting Resolution 2334. His response is included below. It should be noted that pro-Israel groups in New Zealand targeted

Office of Hon Murray McCully

Minister of Foreign Affairs

3 FEB 2017

John Salisbury
jtlsalisbury@hotmail.com

Dear John

Thank you for your correspondence of 26 December 2016 regarding New Zealand's support for United Nations Security Council Resolution 2334.

New Zealand regards itself as a friend to both Israelis and Palestinians. We have for many years been a strong supporter of a negotiated two-state peace deal, and have sought to provide both political and practical support to the parties in reaching such an agreement.

New Zealand's support and co-sponsorship of Resolution 2334 is consistent with our approach to the Israeli-Palestinian conflict over many decades and the statements New Zealand made regularly on this issue during our two year term on the Security Council.

Thank you for taking the time to express your views.

Yours sincerely

Hon Murray McCully
Minister of Foreign Affairs

Mr McCully personally, so getting praise to counteract the abuse is important.

On Thursday 29 December, Australia's Foreign Minister implied that she would have voted 'no' to Resolution 2334, if Australia had been on the UN Security Council. This was a slap in the face to long-time military partners USA, Britain, New Zealand and France who all voted either 'yes' or 'abstain' on the resolution.

On a personal note, the months following the 2016 walk were spent getting my wife's health under control. We have all heard about how debilitating back issues can be. Now I know from first-hand experience.

Disappointing Complicity

AS WE TICKED OVER INTO 2017, WHAT WAS THE OUTLOOK FOR Palestine? In Australia, APAN strengthened and solidified their position as an effective pressure group to advocate for the Palestinian cause with a number of strong initiatives. The Recognise Palestine Walks had all been promoted and endorsed by APAN. However, conversely, the Turnbull government remained enthusiastic cheerleaders of Israel, no matter what Israel did. Donald Trump, as incoming president, did not look encouraging. Prior to running for office he had never shown any interest in issues of justice and human rights. His links to the 'Israel can do no wrong' crowd in American politics was taking shape, especially with mega Republican donor Sheldon Adelson who was the equivalent force within the Republican Party that Haim Saban was within the Democratic Party.

There were defeats and victories, back and forth endlessly, in the battle to end Israel's discrimination against the Palestinians. That was the scenario in Australia in 2017, just like it had been in 2016. A significant defeat for Palestine, and therefore a victory for the Israel lobby, was the invitation extended by the Turnbull government for Israel's Prime Minister Bibi Netanyahu to visit Australia. The invitation was made in 2016 and was significant for two reasons. Firstly, it was the first ever visit to Australia by an Israeli Prime Minister. Secondly, it sent a clear message that Australia would not play by the 'international rules-based order' on this issue. Our Foreign Minister would frequently harangue China about their behaviour in the South China Sea, urging them to abide by the rulings of The Hague Permanent Court of Arbitration. Yet Julie Bishop was curiously not urging Israel to, in a similar vein, abide by the rulings of similar international bodies about their behaviour in the Middle East.

Netanyahu arrived in Sydney and stayed for four days. Two-way trade between the two countries remained modest and the precise purpose of the visit looked opaque. Yet out of the jaws of defeat a modest victory was discerned by those of us yearning for an end to Palestinian suffering. Despite strenuous attempts to ensure the opposite, Israel remains a very controversial country and a lot of dissent surfaced about Mr Netanyahu's visit. The prominent Australian journalist and Vice Chancellor's Fellow at La Trobe University in Melbourne, Tony Walker, neatly summed up by writing, 'Canberra needs not be seen as aligning itself with forces in Israel that disrespect the rule of law, are antagonistic to international conventions and believe in a policy of territorial expansion.' The visit was publicly opposed by 60 prominent Australians. Seldom, if ever, is such a stand taken in objection to a visit by a foreign leader.

Two former Prime Ministers added their voices of concern also. Firstly, Bob Hawke sounded like he would now agree with our petition. He said, in the publicity around Netanyahu's visit, that 'it was time for Australia to recognise Palestine's statehood'. Then Kevin Rudd openly challenged Netanyahu's policies saying, 'The State of Israel and Mr Netanyahu are not co-definitional.' Former Prime Minister Rudd also lambasted the Israeli Prime Minister, saying, 'Multiple negotiations by Clinton, Bush and Obama had been torpedoed by him, often at five minutes to midnight.' Mr Rudd also asked whether Mr Netanyahu would use his visit to apologise to the Australian people for his government using forged Australian passports to facilitate an assassination of a member of Hamas in Dubai.

The response to our petition from Foreign Minister Bishop arrived, as the year before, at five minutes to midnight, in terms of the maximum normal response time. I do not know if all petitions are responded to in this way. However, the cursory, anodyne response to both that year and the previous year's petitions made me feel that Bishop thought we were wasting her time.

In March, American author Ben Ehrenreich came to Australia. Principally he was in the country as a guest at the Adelaide Writers' Festival. In 2016 he wrote a book entitled *The Way to the Spring: Life and Death in Palestine*, in which he chronicled the struggle Palestinians face for basic human rights in the land where they have lived for many generations, especially around the village of Nabi Saleh in the West Bank. Ehrenreich lived amongst the Palestinians on and off for three years. He eloquently writes of their attempt 'to hold on, to decline to consent to one's own eradication, to fight actively or through deceptively simple acts of refusal, against powers far stronger than oneself'. I met Ehrenreich personally when he came to Melbourne on 9 March, speaking at the Prahran Community Centre. It was deeply moving to hear him relate the struggle of brave, resilient people.

Due to the circumstances of the 2016 walk (i.e. my wife's ill health at the very time the project was underway), I had made a commitment of sorts that the walk would not be repeated in 2017. Furthermore, whilst the aim of the project had been achieved (keeping awareness of the issue alive), another petition to the Turnbull government was only going to have marginal impact. All governments are capable of changing their policies in response to public pressure and lobbying (e.g. marriage equality) but on equal treatment for Palestinians the Turnbull government was as deaf as any government on the planet. So in 2017, long distance walks and petitions were not discussed. However, the burning issue of doing something to ameliorate the lot of the Palestinians was never far from my mind.

The 45th President of the United States

In April, President Trump ordered bombing strikes against Syria, as a response to alleged chemical weapon use by Bashar al Assad. The president's use of force was almost universally applauded in the USA, the UK and Australia. It was also well received in Israel which views Syria as somewhat of a regional threat. President Trump appointed his son-in-law Jared Kushner as Senior Advisor to the President, a role that he appeared to have little if any qualification or experience to fulfil. Kushner's main role seemed to be working on 'the ultimate deal' in regards to Middle East peace. What could this pro-Israeli settlements man bring to the negotiating table that would be new, neutral and positive? On this point the whole *raison d'être* of creating a Jewish homeland looked farcical. After all, we constantly hear of Jewish people returning to their homeland after being away from the Hebrew heartland for a couple of millennia. Jared Kushner's wife Ivanka, daughter of the president, was born Christian but converted to the religion of her husband, Judaism. Would she thereafter be thought of as a descendant of the ancient Hebrews? Surely she would not be entitled to immediate citizenship of Israel with all the attendant privileges? The Palestinians who clearly had lived on the land in this part of the planet for a very long time would not have to submit to her greater priority, would they? The Law of Return wasn't really being applied to an 'indigenous people', but rather is being applied to those who converted either long ago or recently to a religious movement. Ivanka Trump seemed to prove this point. Rights to live in the land are not being extended to indigenous Palestinians.

In 2017, not a lot was put on the table in regard to Middle East peace by Mr Kushner. Of course, that was of no concern to the Israeli government who have been comfortable with meaningless talk fests for decades whilst continuing their annexation of more Palestinian land for Jewish settlers from the diaspora (even including Ivanka?). It was difficult to have any faith that Mr Kushner would put forward proposals that would be inimical to his Jewish held faith.

It is quite common for members of the Jewish diaspora to immigrate to the land of Israel, a process called Aliyah. I wonder what the process for identification of one's 'Jewishness' is upon arrival at Tel Aviv Airport? No doubt they have their methods. There are many Jewish people these days who have a completely secular orientation (apparently even Bibi Netanyahu). It must surely be the case that at some point the ancestors of these non-believers were devout. By the same token one cannot, I suppose, apply to become Jewish without religious conversion.

Undertaking long journeys around Australia for Palestinian human rights is one thing. Another thing might be, for one so upset about the issue, to make a journey to Israel/Palestine itself. Some of my Israel supporting friends suggested that in order to have a credible opinion on the issue one must visit Israel. They encouraged me to fly to Tel Aviv so I can see how progressive and hi tech the place is. Some of my friends at APAN have suggested I travel to the West Bank or even Gaza to witness first-hand the suffering and deprivation of Palestinians living under military occupation. At this stage I consider the best use of my resources is to work for change here in Australia.

On 15 May I participated in a solidarity call for Palestinian prisoners of conscience in Israeli prisons. This was to undertake a 24-hour fast called the Salt Water Challenge. No food or liquid except salt water for a 24-hour period. Also during May, President

Trump visited Saudi Arabia. There would be no 'drain the swamp' type changes in American foreign policy here. The new president danced the sword dance with his hosts whilst arranging billions of dollars in arms sales. The feudal monarchy that regularly beheads people, treats women as vassals, and supplied 15 of the 19 World Trade Centre participants of 9/11/2001, received Mr Trump's blessing. Also in May 2017, Iran held democratic (albeit imperfect) elections, but the treatment of Iran by Donald Trump did not match the ardour he displayed towards Saudi Arabia. To be fair, this has been the position of several prior occupants of the White House. It's just that, far from 'draining the swamp', the 45th President seemed to be expanding and deepening the swamp.

This may seem as though it is slightly off topic when writing about a physical and intellectual journey for equal rights for Palestinians. However, it does open one's eyes to consider the larger political ferment within which we live. In Western countries, we constantly hear from our political leaders about how relentlessly they are fighting the scourge of terrorism, in order to protect us. Is that entirely true? Are our political leaders really doing everything in their power to ensure our security? Consider the following example from the UK.

In December 2015, British Prime Minister David Cameron needed the support of the Liberal Democratic Party in the British Parliament to bomb Syria. The leader of the Lib Dems, Tim Farron, told David Cameron that his support for airstrikes would be conditional on the government authorising an enquiry into '...foreign funding and support of terrorist groups in the UK'. According to Farron, Cameron advised that he would discuss his request with the then Home Secretary, Theresa May. A stipulation of Farron's request was that the report be published. Prime Minister Cameron duly went ahead with the report which was completed by the spring of 2016. However, Cameron and May reneged on their commitment to release the report, as its findings were sensitive. Up until the time of writing, the report into 'external funding of terror in the UK' has not seen the light of day. Tim Farron said:

> 'It is a scandal that the government are suppressing the report. The only conclusion you can draw is that they are worried about what it actually says. We hear regularly about Saudi arms deals or ministers going to Riyadh to kowtow to their royal family but yet our government will not release a report that will clearly criticise Saudi Arabia. All this government seems to care about is cosying up to one of the most extreme, nasty and oppressive regimes in the world. You would think our security would be more important but it appears not. For that Theresa May should be ashamed of herself.'

It should be noted that in 2018 Saudi Arabia and Israel have developed some sort of relationship, based on their mutual enmity with Iran. Also worth mentioning is that, as of 2018, around 80% of Conservative MPs are members of a group called Conservative Friends of Israel.

Further 2017 Events

In late July I attended a two-day conference in Sydney entitled 'BDS: Driving Global Justice for Palestine'. The conference was held at Sydney University, under the auspices of Sydney Staff for BDS, APAN and several other Palestinian support groups. It was real nourishment for the brain and soul for those of us involved in the quest for Palestinian freedom. The main plenary session hosted the well-known Palestinian American writer Yousef Munayyer. He is the Executive Director of the US campaign for Palestinian Rights.

Predictably, there was an attempt by the Anti-Defamation League to pressure Sydney University into not allowing the event to even take place. I wrote to Sydney University Vice Chancellor Michael Spence, thanking him for allowing the conference to go ahead. He replied, 'Thank you for your message and support. The University is committed to academic freedom and that we ought to be a forum for the respectful discussion of ideas, even those that some find difficult.'

The Sydney Uni BDS Conference was held, coincidentally, at the same time as the NSW Labor Party Conference was held at Sydney Town Hall. Speared by the redoubtable Bob Carr, a motion was passed urging the next federal ALP government to recognise Palestine. It was a terrific initiative and one mirrored by similar motions at Queensland and ACT Labor Party conferences. Progress along the path to speaking the truth about a long running injustice was being made, it seemed.

On 27 August the APAN Annual Fundraiser was held. The event alternates yearly between Melbourne and Sydney. As in previous years, the event was held at Aurora Receptions in East Brunswick. Speakers from all sides of politics at the federal level were present. During her speech the Co-Convenor of the Parliamentary Friends of Palestine, Maria Vamvakinou, specifically mentioned the impact that the two walks for Palestine projects had made and even asked if I was contemplating another! This further made me realise that being a friend of Palestine in Canberra is not the easiest road to walk. Ms Vamvakinou really seemed to appreciate the act of solidarity that we had made by undertaking the walks. Any act of solidarity we in the 'laity' can provide is important because the pro-Israel lobby will attempt to isolate and humiliate politicians. Conversely, being a friend of Israel will make your life easier. You will not feel any heat whilst being relaxed or neutral about the Palestinian situation. You will not be targeted for ad hominem attacks.

In September I took my wife to Europe for her first ever visit. Whilst in France we went to the French Resistance Museum in Lyon. The museum graphically depicts the difficult conditions faced by the French in the years 1940–1945. Defeated militarily by Germany, most French accepted foreign control via the Vichy government. However, some were determined to resist and they formed militant groups called the Maquis. They tried to make life uncomfortable for the occupying forces. It was a brutal struggle. The Maquis were assisted by Britain, who provided arms and equipment.

New Zealand–Australian woman Nancy Wake was part of the Maquis. She was highly decorated with medals from many countries after the war. Similarly, Irish author Samuel Beckett was active with Maquis in sabotage operations against the German army. I'm sure the Germans called the Maquis 'terrorists'. What would we call them? Certainly in today's France the Maquis are celebrated as heroes. What is different about Palestinians taking up arms against an occupying army? That is the question to which we are awaiting an answer.

Wandering the streets of Berlin a couple of weeks later, I noticed numerous little brass plaques inset into the footpaths of the German capital. The plaques denote the location and homes from which Jewish Germans were removed and transported to concentration camps. It is a worthy gesture to mark an undoubted wrong. I wonder whether in a future Israel there will be brass plaques inserted into pavements commemorating the 400 Palestinian villages that were obliterated in 1948 Palestine? Perhaps that could be added as a postscript to future editions of the famous Leon Uris book. In years to come, will we feel differently about those Palestinians who took up arms against their military occupier? Or is it only sometimes right and just to take up arms against an occupying army?

Whilst overseas in September 2017, I had reason to write to former judge of the High Court of Australia Michael Kirby. Many Australians have great respect and admiration for former Justice Kirby. He is a great champion for human rights both locally and globally. The reason I wrote to him was because of an interview he gave to the *Australian Jewish News* newspaper. According to an article written by journalist Michael Brull in *New Matilda* magazine, former Justice Kirby expressed his good feelings towards two Israeli judges Moshe Landau and Aharon Barak, whom he was friends with. Brull took issue with the two Israeli judges for their rulings on human rights for Palestinians. A copy of the exchange is recorded below.

-----Original Message-----
From: John Salisbury [mailto:jtlsalisbury@hotmail.com]
Sent: Tuesday, September 12, 2017 5:41 PM
To: mail@michaelkirby.ccm.au
Subject: Jewish News

Dear Justice Kirby

You don't know me and I hope you do not find it rude of me to write to you out of the blue.

The reason for my contacting you is because of an article in The Jewish News. I am overseas at present so cannot read the article. I have however read an online piece by Michael Brull in New Matilda. Have you read Michael Brull's article?

The Jewish News may have selectively quoted you or edited your remarks.

Many of us regard you as a strong champion of human rights internationally.

Can we make an exception for Israel? They continually flout United Nations resolutions and rulings of the International Court of Justice. The suffering of the defenceless Palestinians as they endure occupation is a shame for humanity.

With respect and admiration
Yours sincerely

John Salisbury

From: Michael Kirby <mail@michaelkirby.com.au>
Sent: Thursday, 14 September 2017 4:15 PM
To: 'John Salisbury'
Subject: RE: Jewish News

Dear John Salisbury,

No need to apologise. Sorry to take the time to respond. I have been engaged in many things.

I have not read Michael Brull's article. Before your letter I did not know that it existed.

I do not agree that Israel, or any other country, can have exceptions from the application of international human rights law. I agree that the Palestinian people are entitled to the protection of international human rights law and to the exercise of the people's right to self-determination, promised by that law.

I did not intend by expressing my good feelings towards old judicial friends from Israel (Moshe Landau and Aaron Barack) to buy into only partly understood controversies about both men. I have received another letter of complaint seeking to involve me in those controversies. As you might understand, I have enough controversies on my hands (North Korea, access to essential healthcare against pharmaceutical patents and LGBTIQ rights) without involuntarily buying into the controversies of the Middle East. I was merely describing these 2 men as I had met them and as their attitudes about the rule of law impressed me. Of course, I might be right or I might be wrong about them. But I do not have time at the moment to get deeply into the controversies.

If you feel that my reported remarks are in some way inadequate or distorted, by all means express your views to Australian Jewish News.

With all good wishes,

Michael Kirby

The Hon. Michael Kirby AC CMG,
Level 7, 195 Macquarie Street,
SYDNEY   NSW   2000
AUSTRALIA
Telephone: 61 2 9231 5830
Fax: 61 2 9231 5811
Email: mail@michaelkirby.com.au

The crucial point made by former Justice Kirby is, 'I do not agree that Israel, or any other country, can have exceptions from the application of human rights law. I agree that the Palestinian people are entitled to the protection of international human rights law and to the exercise of the peoples' right to self-determination, promised by that law.'

Back in Australia in October, another example of anti-Palestinian prejudice came to light at the 100th Anniversary of the

Australian Light Horse charge at Beersheba. The celebration saw a re-enactment of the military action by descendants of the former brigade. The occasion was, in my view, hijacked by Israel for dubious purposes. After all, there was no such country as Israel in 1917 and the Australian Light Horse were fighting the Ottoman Empire as subjects of the British Empire.

Embarrassingly, our Prime Minister went along with the fiction that somehow the Light Horse had a role in Israel's formation. An insert in *The Weekend Australian* newspaper was instructive in this regard. The insert, entitled 'Beersheba, Legend of the Light Horse', was fronted on page one by an opinion piece by Malcolm Turnbull called 'Our Unbreakable Bond'. He was referring to the unbreakable bond between Australia and Israel! Prime Minister Turnbull also referred to the 'shared values' of Israel and Australia.

Printed with kind permission from David Pope

Campaigns to deny Palestinians their basic rights come to our attention almost monthly. Israeli attempts to turn antipathy to sympathy never take a holiday. Israel's chief concern is to maintain positive relations with Western governments. This is no easy task considering the militaristic nature of the Likud government and the wide use of social media to record the awful behaviour of Israeli soldiers in the occupied territories. However, outside advocates in Western legislatures are cultivated, as the following example illustrates.

In December, a British Conservative MP, Priti Patel, was forced to resign over some inappropriate contact with Israel. Ms Patel, a British-born person of Indian descent, was appointed International Development Secretary by Prime Minister Theresa May in July 2016. In November 2017, it was revealed that Patel, whilst on holiday in Israel in August 2017, had several meetings with Israeli government officials, without telling the Foreign Office or even British Embassy officials in Tel Aviv. Among other things, one of the recommendations she made following the trip was for Britain to give international aid money to field hospitals run by the Israeli army in the Israeli-occupied Golan Heights region of Syria. Apparently that was the best way for Britain to spend its international development budget. It came as no surprise, however, as Patel is an ardent and unwavering supporter of Israel and a member of the Conservative Friends of Israel. Back in October 2016, she instructed her Department for International Aid to review aid given to Palestine through the UN agencies and the Palestinian Authority. Changes to the way aid was given were made that thrilled supporters of Israel including the Jewish Leadership Council and the Zionist Federation. She was like putty in their hands. Along with her ardent support of Israel, Patel had a rolled gold conservative/reactionary position on economic and social issues. For example, until very recently, she was in favour of reintroduction of the death penalty, as well as being an advocate for the alcohol and tobacco industries in the UK. Unfortunately for Patel, her week-long round of secret meetings with officials (including Bibi Netanyahu) in Israel was outside ministerial guidelines and once her activities were revealed she was sacked by Prime Minister May. These days, the more conservative and right-wing politicians are, the more likely they will be to cuddle up to Likud Israel.

In November, AFOPA (Australian Friends of Palestine Association) brought Israeli journalist Gideon Levy to Australia. The renowned *Haaretz* newspaper writer spoke at the Edward Said Memorial lecture at the University of Adelaide. Levy spoke at a number of subsequent venues around Australia. I went to a very packed auditorium in Melbourne where he spoke. He talked about, wryly, a meeting he'd had at Parliament House in Canberra with our Foreign Minister Julie Bishop. The 'off the record' meeting was polite but Levy said that 'her position on the Palestinian issue wouldn't shame any Israeli right-wing leader'.

This was confirmation, if it was needed, that the Recognise Palestine Walks had no influence whatsoever on her outlook. The Israeli journalist said he 'could easily understand why Netanyahu felt so comfortable on his visit here last February', adding that 'even hard-right Israeli politician Bezalel Smotrich would feel at home here'. Smotrich is a devoutly religious Member of the Israeli Knesset who believes that Palestinians in the West Bank have three options: 'To leave, accept rule by a Jewish state, or fight and be defeated.'

In spite of Julie Bishop's response to our petition that 'the Australian government is a strong supporter of a two-state solution', the harsh reality is that both Netanyahu and Israeli politicians like Bezalel Smotrich are opposed to a two-state solution. That is why Israel would be apoplectic if Australia were to recognise a Palestinian state, as most members of the Australian Labor Party are in favour of doing. Sweden recognised Palestine in 2014. To demonstrate Israel's disapproval of this, in 2015 Swedish Foreign Minister Margot Wallstrom had to cancel a planned trip to Israel as no Israeli official was prepared to receive her.

This book, as stated at the outset, relates a journey. Both a physical one and one of the mind and heart. On that journey there are peaks and valleys. There are days when you think progress is being made and days when all hope seems to be lost. As much as Gideon Levy spoke inspirationally about the need to keep international pressure on Israel, just a week or so later a deep valley on the journey presented itself. On 6 December, President Trump announced that he will move the USA Embassy from Tel Aviv to Jerusalem. One has to wonder why he would bother to issue such a decree. After all, wasn't his agenda to 'make America great again'? Moving the embassy hardly fitted that agenda. On the other hand, many of his powerful financial backers, such as Sheldon Adelson, had that item near the top of their wish list (the other item was for USA to pull out of the Iran deal) for the Trump presidency.

On 19 December 2017, a United Nations Security Council resolution called for the reversal of Donald Trump's decision to declare Jerusalem as Israel's capital. Every one of the Security Council members except the USA backed the resolution. Being a permanent member of the Security Council, America vetoed the resolution. This was done enthusiastically by Ambassador Nikki Haley who seemed to take her role as dual-purpose...America *and* Israel's ambassador to the UN!

On 22 December, the same resolution came before the UN General Assembly. Nikki Haley issued a direct threat, saying that the US would think twice about funding the world body if it voted to condemn President Trump's decision. 128 countries voted in favour of the resolution, 35 abstained, and just 9 voted 'no'. It is worth mentioning the 7 countries that supported Israel and the USA. They were Guatemala, Honduras, Togo, Micronesia (pop. 104,000), Marshall Islands (pop. 53,000), Palau (pop. 21,000) and Nauru (pop. 13,000). Australia abstained.

As 2017 drew to a close, we waited and waited for any details of the 'deal of the century' that Trump had spoken of with regard to the Israel/Palestine conflict. Previous American presidents approached the issue with almost unequivocal endorsement of a 'two-state solution'. Would the 45th president support it too? In reality, the two-state solution is on life-support because Israeli settlement expansion has made a contiguous State of Palestine almost impossible (there would need to be a land bridge between the West Bank and Gaza, for example). Plus Israel cheekily insists on conditions that no sovereign state could agree to (e.g. no capacity for a Palestinian state to defend itself). So, if the two-state solution to the problem is past, what becomes the position of the United States (and Australia)? Should Bezalel Smotrich's solution, as outlined above, be the way forward? Or should the area between the Mediterranean Sea and the Jordan River become a one-state democracy with full political rights for all inhabitants?

2017 passed as another year with no improvement in the situation for Palestinians and numerous storm clouds on the horizon. It seemed that the pain endured by them rolled on endlessly. The Australian government intoned regularly about Australia being a country that embraced the concept of 'the rule of law', and that 'justice must be blind', as well as the idea that 'no man is above the law'. This was all uttered with chest-thumping pride. Our Foreign Minister frequently used the phrase 'the international rules-based order' when speaking of Chinese activities in the South China Sea (China rejected the ruling of the Permanent Court of Arbitration regarding territorial disputes with neighbouring countries in the South China Sea). However, when international bodies such as the UN or the International Court of Justice made resolutions or rulings concerning Israel, Australia treated them with the contempt they did not deserve. Israel was immune to the dictates of international institutions and was supported in doing so by America and by Australia. When you are a regional superpower backed to the hilt by a global superpower, apparently you can do whatever you like. China was following that course of action and ignoring the Permanent Court of Arbitration's ruling. That is what powerful countries do.

My heart ached for the long-suffering Palestinians, as the 50-year anniversary of the occupation of the West Bank came and went with the daily humiliations of checkpoints unmitigated. The blatant discrimination based on your religion or ethnicity was intact. Were he alive, how would Leon Uris feel today, I wondered? If his book was anything to go by, probably fine. Blind loyalty to one's tribe can be a powerful affliction. Leon Uris was of that ilk.

The only glimmer of hope was with the strategy that Marcelo Svirsky so passionately argued for in 2014: BDS. BDS is a campaign to ask the world to not have normal relations with Israel until it adjusts its behaviour. The campaign began in 2005, led by 170 civil/societal organisations in Palestine. After all, the refusal of sporting teams and entertainers to play in South Africa was highly instrumental in ending the system of apartheid in the 1970s and 1980s. Perhaps Israel would come to its senses after a similar policy was employed to end the injustices in Palestine.

In late 2017, *The Australian* newspaper's Middle East correspondent, John Lyons, released a memoir about the six years he had spent covering events from 2009 to 2015. Lyons is a very well respected journalist and the book was a no-holds-barred account of his experiences. Entitled *Balcony over Jerusalem*, the book deals with all the events of the region during his time there: The Arab Spring, the fall of Colonel Gaddafi in Libya and also Iran, Syria and Lebanon. However, the largest part of the book deals with Israel/Palestine. Especially interesting to read about was the way his stories were received by sections of the Jewish community in Australia. Like Antony Loewenstein before him, Lyons endured nasty verbal assaults. I quote, 'I was coming to realise that when you write about Israel you are open to a level of abuse that I had never seen before. As a journalist, you quickly learn that you could have a very pleasant life if you wrote what Israel wanted you to.'

Over the six years of living in Jerusalem, John Lyons, together with his wife and son, witnessed the reality of Israel's occupation of the West Bank and Gaza up close and in person on numerous occasions. He even persuaded arch Israel supporter and funder of politicians' visits to Israel, Australian businessman Albert Dadon, to accompany him on a visit to Hebron in December 2010. Seeing the realities of occupation up close was a wake-up call for Dadon, apparently. He said, 'It opened my eyes. This is a dark side of a society that you don't want to face but when you face it you come out more informed. What I saw that day was not Jewish.' *Balcony over Jerusalem* is a balanced and honest account of Israel/Palestine. The chapter entitled 'Frankenstein's Monster' is the most relentlessly depressing 38 pages you will ever read as it describes the 'monster' of occupation.

The reality of the occupation is infinitely worse than the public realises: 'If the whole world could see the occupation up close, it would demand that it end tomorrow. Israel's treatment of the Palestinians would not pass muster if the full details were known' (John Lyons, *Balcony over Jerusalem*, p. 366).

Lyons also ponders the broader geopolitical implications of the West's (Australia included) reluctance to insist that Israel complies with the 'international rules-based order'. He writes that, 'When China begins colonising the South China Sea, can the world object? Either international law applies across the board or it is a free-for-all survival of the fittest.'

An Australian who lived in Israel at much the same time as *The Australian* newspaper Middle East correspondent John Lyons was Dave Sharma. Sharma was appointed Australia's Ambassador to Israel from 2013 to 2017. Sharma appeared to find nothing controversial about Israel. Amazingly enough, our man in Tel Aviv turned into an enthusiastic Israelophile, lauding the 70-year-old country at every possible opportunity. This was especially surprising seeing as some of his predecessors in the role have been much more guarded in their praise. One previous ambassador, Dr Ross Burns, even became, after his time in Tel Aviv, an executive board member of APAN. More than that, polls indicate that the Australian public is sympathetic to the Palestinian cause, so for Sharma to 'go rogue' with his embrace of all things Israeli is perhaps unprofessional.

I have heard that the most written about figure in history (in terms of the number of biographies) is Napoleon Bonaparte. That has nothing to do with our issue here except that, similarly, a huge number of books have been written about the Palestinian issue. No other issue over the past 70 years has attracted more debates, more reports, more documentaries. Amazing numbers of people with large, enriched cranium material have devoted their minds to resolving this problem. All to no avail largely, except that we now know, increasingly, the parameters of the injustice. When luminaries such as President Jimmy Carter and Archbishop Desmond Tutu refer to Israel's policies in the West Bank as apartheid, it has significant effect because they come to the issue with an objective perspective. Special praise, however, must be given to Jewish activists like Norman Finkelstein, Ilan Pappé and Anna Baltzer. Along with many others, they have devoted many decades of their lives to educating us about the historical realities of the Zionist state. These people have become almost heroic figures because they cannot be fobbed off or taken down by bluster or bravado or by false accusations of anti-Semitism that are the go-to weapon used against those of us who refuse to consign Palestinians to the dustbin of history.

Artists Stand Up

In early January 2018, there was some good news. New Zealand singer Lorde announced that she was cancelling the Tel Aviv concerts included in her upcoming tour. Lorde made the decision to not play in Israel after representations made to her by two New Zealand women – one of Palestinian heritage, the other Jewish. In the larger context, the BDS campaign has been going since 2005. It is a campaign initiated by 170 Palestinian civil and society bodies asking entertainers, sportspeople and businesspeople to sanction Israel by withdrawing their contact until Israel behaves itself and complies with international laws and ends the occupation. Lorde would not be the first to undertake such a principled stand. Others include Roger Waters, Elvis Costello and Lauryn Hill. Many more have ignored the call, however. Predictably, Lorde would feel the wrath of those upset with her decision. American Rabbi Shmuley Boteach took out a full page advertisement in the *Washington Post* newspaper, calling her a 'bigot' and stating that her decision was part of 'a global anti-Semitic boycott of Israel'. For good measure, Rabbi Boteach gave her a dose of 'whataboutism' by noting that Lorde would continue with concerts in Russia 'despite Putin's support for Assad's genocidal regime'.

In April, Lorde's decision not to play in Israel was matched by Natalie Portman. The Jerusalem-born actress had in 2017 been awarded the Genesis prize. The prize has been in existence since 2012 and is awarded to Jewish people who have 'attained recognition and excellence in their fields and who inspire others through their engagement and dedication to the Jewish community and/or the

State of Israel.' Portman announced in April that she would not attend the award ceremony scheduled for July. That was a slap in the face of significant proportions to those involved in awarding the prize. Portman's spokesperson said, 'Recent events in Israel had been extremely distressing to her and she does not feel comfortable participating in any public events in Israel.' Portman also mentioned her 'reluctance to share a stage with Israeli Prime Minister Bibi Netanyahu and therefore appear to be endorsing him'.

In August, American singer and songwriter Lana Del Rey cancelled the Israel show that was booked as part of her world tour. She was to be one of the headline acts of the Meteor Festival in September 2018. Following her announcement, a number of other acts scheduled to perform at the festival also withdrew. Is there a financial inducement for artists to play in Israel over and above other venues? Certainly ticket prices are very high in Tel Aviv. So taking a principled stand as these artists have done is praiseworthy.

It has often surprised me that of all the iconic rock bands of my formative years the one that shines out as being the most concerned about issues of injustice today is Pink Floyd. Specifically, their chief songwriter Roger Waters. He has spoken out on the issue of Palestine for many years. Waters toured Australia in February and during his visit agreed to a public event sponsored by the wonderful people at APAN. The Q and A style event was hosted by Antony Loewenstein and Randa Abdel-Fattah. Regretfully, I could not attend due to family commitments but Waters spoke powerfully and passionately about the Palestinian cause. I watched a video of the event later on social media. Waters encouraged and applauded the 500 or so audience for their efforts to not hide from the racism and apartheid that is modern Israel. He mentioned the significant shift in opinion on the issue in the US, especially amongst young Jews. That gave him hope. He said that Sheldon Adelson and other oligarchs had to spend increasing millions to counteract the global effort to demand human rights for Palestinians. First this man dazzles us with his music. Now he dazzles us with his activism. Waters is deeply inspirational.

The year 2018 came and went with no improvement in the lives of the persecuted Palestinians. In fact, their misery only intensified. However, some events that took place over the year are worth recording, as part of the long campaign for justice. Also, another walk down here in Australia took place. Let's look back at what transpired.

The Gaza Fence

In March, the Palestinians living in Gaza began protests near the fence that Israel has erected to permanently imprison them. Israel likes to speak of these protests as being attempts by Palestinians to illegally enter Israel. As such, the Israelis say they are allowed to 'defend their border'. The chutzpah of such statements is jaw dropping. Israel has no defined borders. They regard Mandatory Palestine as completely their territory, which is why they consistently pay no regard to UN rulings regarding settlements. Jewish Israelis safeguarded by the might of the IDF can go wherever they like. For example, would the same people who shot and killed unarmed protesters this year near Gaza think that it was perfectly fine for the Israeli settlement of Gush Katif to exist near the Gaza border with Egypt (1967–2005)? Casualties during the Great March of Return numbered more than 200. Men, women and children. The number of wounded and maimed reached 18,000. Medical staff in the coastal enclave of Gaza complained that there was a shortage of prostheses. Israeli snipers picked off their targets at will.

We should never forget the appalling conditions that Gazans are forced to live under as a result of the 12-year blockade Israel has imposed. There is no movement in or out of Gaza without Israeli military control. By land, sea or air. Yet we are supposed to support the nuclear armed state as though they are the victims. There is no 'border'. There is only a perimeter fence that entraps the poor Palestinians in a massive open-air concentration camp.

Moving America's Embassy and Other Transgressions

In May, President Donald Trump moved the US embassy from Tel Aviv to Jerusalem. This was another kick in the teeth for the Palestinians. At least Sheldon Adelson, the largest Republican Party donor, was pleased. Maybe Trump was simply living by a sort of bastardisation of the 'golden rule'. Instead of 'doing unto others', the new golden rule appears to be 'whoever has the gold, he makes the rules'. In one respect it was simply being honest that America took this step. Despite assertions to the contrary, the US has never really been an honest broker between the two parties. The bias towards Israel was evident for many years. Either via the huge number of evangelical Christians who support Israel for religious reasons or via the wealthy and powerful pro-Israel lobby called AIPAC. Also in May, Donald Trump buckled to the demands of his campaign financiers and withdrew from the Iran nuclear deal known as the JCPOA (Joint Comprehensive Plan of Action). This was a policy implementation of former President Barack Obama and was struck between Iran, America, China, Russia, France and the EU. The deal was designed to bring Iran back into the fold of trading nations and remove sanctions, in return for Iran not engaging in any activity to build nuclear weapons. In the lead-up to Trump's decision, both Britain and France tried to counsel him against such a move. He didn't listen. He did listen to Bibi Netanyahu, who expressed delight at the withdrawal. Once again, a demonstration that tiny

Israel seems to have more influence on Middle East issues than its size would indicate.

Looking back on my diary, even at this early part of the year I could feel my anger and frustration welling up. My diary note reads, 'Mulling over another walk! Don't mention it to anyone!' No doubt a reference to my wife. There always seemed to be something highlighting the egregious nature of the occupation. It became like an 'injustice du jour' either in Palestine itself or in one of the countries that were countenancing support for the struggle.

The case of Ahed Tamimi was so typical. This brave young Palestinian girl was jailed in December last year for slapping an Israeli soldier. Israeli soldiers were in the front yard of her home. The 17-year-old was dealing with the situation of her 16-year-old cousin Mohammed who had been shot in the face with a rubber coated steel bullet earlier in the day, and was fighting for his life in hospital. For confronting the uninvited Israeli soldiers who were on her family property, she was later arrested and sentenced to eight months' prison by a military tribunal. An example of justice Israeli style. At the same time in America, those who spoke out for Palestinian justice, especially on university campuses, were targeted for punishment in terms of their future employment prospects. The cases of Norman Finkelstein and Steven Salaita adequately demonstrate this.

There were irritations galore in the 'respected' newspapers of record. *The Australian* newspaper published a ghastly piece by Daniel Pipes (an American pro-Israel commentator) in which he called for Israel to inflict a crushing military defeat against Palestinians. As if they hadn't been crushed enough already. In May 2018, even the respected news magazine *The Economist* got in on the act by publishing an article entitled 'Gaza's Ruthless Pragmatist'. The article was about a gentleman named Yahya Sinwar and it described him as a possible future leader. However, the piece concluded with this charming paragraph:

'But if Mr Sinwar aspires to lead the Palestinians, he cannot do so at the helm of an armed group. The world will not recognise Hamas until it renounces violence.'

One might suggest that General Cornwallis would likely have made the same demand of General George Washington. Throughout history armed struggle has been part of many movements for freedom and self-determination. I do not endorse Hamas per se. Their methods in Gaza are akin to a police state, I am told. I would not endorse them any more than I would have endorsed the Jewish armed militias such as the Haganah, Irgun or Lehi, that were so extravagantly praised by Leon Uris. Having said that, I do strongly endorse the Palestinians' struggle for freedom, and how is that to be achieved? The concept consistently put forward by the likes of Bibi Netanyahu is that acts of terror are bred into the DNA of Palestinians. That is not believable. Palestinians do not have F-16s, Apache helicopters and nuclear weapons like Israel, so they must choose from a narrow list of options. Perhaps they seek to emulate the 1930–40 Jewish militias and their success (before they had a national army and sophisticated weapons) over the British. Upon investigation I learnt that *The Economist*'s Jerusalem correspondent is a man by the name of Anshel Pfeffer. He is a British-Israeli dual national. As such he is hardly dispassionate and balanced. One might ask when Israel will be asked to renounce violence?

On his Twitter page Mr Pfeffer frequently bemoans the supposed rise in anti-Semitism now besetting the British Labour Party along with many other British-born people of the Jewish faith. On and on the attacks went throughout the first six months of 2018. Palestinians were actually dying during the same period but journalists such as Mr Pfeffer did not consider it worthy of outrage or even concern. Anti-Semitism within the British Labour Party was *the* evil of our time and page after page was written condemning Jeremy Corbyn and demanding his removal as Labour Party leader. Unlike the

British Conservative party, where up to 80% of parliamentary members belong to 'Conservative Friends of Israel', Jeremy Corbyn has always been a supporter of Palestine. *Quelle horreur* if he were ever to become Prime Minister.

It hardly needs to be said that any racism or discrimination against those of different, colour, background, ethnicity or religion is abhorrent in Britain, and everywhere else. But isn't that what is happening in Palestine? Isn't that a much more egregious example of discrimination? So remarkable to plainly see that those who for so long endured discrimination are now perpetuating it themselves.

Anshel Pfeffer and his ilk were persistent in their attempts to divert attention away from Israel and the occupation. Their efforts were two-pronged. On the one hand they sought to demonise the people they were occupying. In other words, Fatah and especially Hamas were the problem. 'If only they were reasonable people we could have fixed this problem long ago...' was the argument put forward. Secondly, they attacked anyone in the West who was concerned about the dreadful situation of the Palestinians in the West Bank and Gaza. Such people were slandered for voicing concerns and the weapon was a rather effective one. It wasn't that such people were genuine in their concerns over the fate of Palestinians. That would not be accepted at all. No, such people were just using the fate of the Palestinians as a vehicle with which to display their real agenda, anti-Semitism. A convenient but implausible argument (to say the very least). Too often media stories in Australia, and especially in Britain, seemed comfortable to make anti-Semitism the issue rather than justice for Palestinians.

The Idea for Another Walk

There are many reasons to note the significant contribution of the Greens Party in the Australian political realm. They set the benchmark in many areas. For example, they are the most progressive party on: humane treatment of refugees; election campaign financing; a federal ICAC; a royal commission into the financial services industry; and climate change. On most of these issues, the Labor Party will eventually 'catch up' and embrace the same positions. On Palestine too the Greens were out in front. They already had recognition of Palestine in their policy platform. Would the Labor Party 'catch up' on this issue too? Many Labor party members were already supportive of the Palestinian cause although there were notable 'come what may' supporters of Israel too. Polls in 2018 consistently showed Labor in front of the Coalition and the likelihood of a change of government in 2019 grew as the 2018 calendar year progressed. Labor had a very good chance of being the next government whenever the next federal election took place.

The triennial Labor Party Conference would be held in Adelaide in July. Bob Carr and Queensland Labor Vice-President Wendy Turner had lobbied long and hard for Palestinian recognition. Wendy Turner was also a member of the APAN Executive Board. In early May, I was toying with the idea of another walk for Palestine. It would be from Melbourne to Adelaide and as part of a push for Palestinian recognition by the ALP. I emailed APAN President Bishop George Browning to run the idea past him. He did not dissuade me. His view was that every bit of advocacy would help. With some trepidation I broached the subject with my wife.

Surprisingly, she was not very upset. Perhaps she was expecting it. She knows me too well. The very day we spoke about it, America symbolically opened the new US embassy in Jerusalem. The new embassy would have to await construction but a ceremony unveiling of a nameplate took place. President Trump did not attend. Maybe that was appropriate because most of those in attendance were American Jewish. Jared Kushner and his convert wife Ivanka Trump, Ambassador Friedman and Sheldon Adelson. On the same day, 55 unarmed Gazans were shot by Israeli snipers at the separation fence. 2000 were injured. That was motivation, if any was needed, to undertake some further advocacy.

The Melbourne to Adelaide walk had logistical problems that made the endeavour difficult. It would take almost one month of walking to cover the 737 kilometres. On previous walks from Sydney to Canberra the distance was a much shorter 347 kilometres and there were nice spaces from town to town that could be walked in a day. That was not the case this time around. Either my wife would need to accompany me in a support vehicle, or I would need to carry a tent. I spent several days working out the route and the accommodation. We phoned Wendy Turner who, like fellow board member of APAN Bishop Browning, was positive about me doing the walk. After a day or two of consideration, my wonderful wife agreed to join me in the project. She would drive alongside me in a support car.

The Labor Party gathering in Adelaide was to take place 26–28 July. Therefore, our departure from Melbourne would need to be late June. We purchased various items of clothing to combat the wind, rain and cold that we would no doubt encounter at that time of year. I made the various accommodation bookings. Mostly Bed and Breakfast, but lots of motels, country pubs and caravan parks too. I paid another visit to the shop that provided banners. RJS Pty Ltd would also design decals for our car. The project was coming together. A physical training regime was implemented, as in previous years.

On 24 May it was announced by Speaker Tony Smith that the five by-elections for the House of Representatives would be held on 28 July. This set in motion an unusually long campaigning period. Some suggested that the choice of such a date was done deliberately so as to interfere with the ALP Conference (scheduled for 26–28 July). This might have meant that important resources and personnel would not be able to campaign. At any rate, the ALP leadership group advised that the triennial conference would be postponed. This put a huge spanner in the works of our project. I cancelled all the accommodation reservations that I had made. I requested refunds for the 16 bed and breakfast bookings we had made.

On 31 May we heard that the conference was rescheduled for 16–18 December. We put our project on hold, however. The federal political scene was in a state of flux and some commentators thought an early election was on the cards. Both major parties campaigned vigorously for the two marginal seats of Longman and Braddon. Malcolm Turnbull saw implications for the return of the Coalition at the next General Election in the result. If either of those two marginal seats had been won by the Coalition, the PM might have called a General Election before Christmas. There was no point in having the ALP Conference under those circumstances.

The long campaign brought no joy for the Coalition as the results came in on the night of 28 July. Two of the seats were safe Labor electorates, and so they remained, increasing their majority. The third of the five electorates was for Mayo in South Australia, held by Rebekha Sharkie (Centre Alliance). She easily held off a challenge by Alexander Downer's daughter Georgina. Importantly, the two marginal seats of Braddon, in Tasmania, and Longman, in Queensland, stayed Labor (with swings to Labor).

A few short weeks later, the governing Liberal Party changed their leader and therefore Prime Minister. I was amazed at the lengths to which people will go to exact some sort of revenge (i.e. Tony Abbott and Barnaby Joyce), but that is not a matter to discuss here. These political events were germane, however, to the 'if and when' of our walk for Palestine.

With the leadership change complete, the now former Prime Minister Malcolm Turnbull did as he promised and resigned from Parliament. Interestingly, the Liberal Party chose as its candidate to replace him the former Australian Ambassador to Israel, Dave Sharma. Unfortunately for Mr Sharma, a high-profile local doctor, Kerryn Phelps, chose to contest Wentworth as well. During the course of the campaign, the concern of this tome was suddenly thrust into the spotlight. New Prime Minister Scott Morrison, on 16 October, called a press conference and declared that he was 'considering' a move of Australia's embassy in Israel from Tel Aviv to Jerusalem. Although it was unprincipled and unwise, Scott Morrison's announcement only served to highlight the issue of Palestine. It gave even more logic and reason for our project to proceed.

The issue of Israel/Palestine was alive and kicking in the Australian political ferment. Not only amongst those of us who were doing our best to ameliorate the suffering and oppression on the Palestinian side. There are many Australians, Jewish and non-Jewish, who consider it their duty to prosecute the case for Israel. Such people are not merely content with the ethnically privileged state that now exists. Many of them work to entrench that position. Australia moving its embassy would be a small but useful step in cementing the international bias in favour of the Jewish state. It is a 'tribute' to the Jewish population of Australia, on whose behalf the pro-Israel lobby purport to speak, that they have such influence as to have Scott Morrison make such an announcement. After all, the Jewish community comprise only around one half of one per cent of the Australian population. A similar, or even greater, influence appears to exist in the USA. President Trump had already moved its embassy to Jerusalem.

In a similar vein, Morrison declared on 16 October that Australia would review its support of the JCPOA regarding Iran. This was another policy change that was driven by an excessive and unprincipled desire to appease Trump, Israel and the pro-Israel lobby in Australia. Naturally enough, the media considered this announcement as a way of trying to shore up the Jewish vote in Wentworth (10–12% of this affluent area is Jewish). However, Scott Morrison was amenable to candidate Dave Sharma's suggestion because at base both men are ardent supporters of Israel.

Our project still had an uncertain gestation because it was not clear what ramifications a loss in Wentworth would have for the government. It would mean a minority government. Would the Prime Minister be obliged to call an early election? As the campaign ground on, the independent Kerryn Phelps proved herself to be an effective and appealing candidate. Around this time, we heard from noted psephologist Antony Green that, even if the Liberals lost in Wentworth, the Morrison government would still be able to cling to power. On 20 October Kerryn Phelps won the Wentworth by-election. Our decision, with still a little trepidation around the bubbling political cauldron, was made soon afterwards. The walk to Adelaide was on.

Training recommenced in earnest. I informed my friends at APAN. They were happy to sponsor me and use the project in their advocacy towards the Labor Party. We began re-booking accommodation for the numerous towns between Melbourne and Adelaide. My wife put aside her misgivings and agreed to accompany me. I was full of love and admiration for her. She only suggested that we take our little dog with us. No objection from me about that. It did mean some difficulties with overnight accommodation but we could get by. In previous walks from Sydney to Canberra I had a few sleepless nights leading up to the event. Planning had to be done carefully as I was going to be out there on the road alone. This time would be different because a support vehicle was going to be right there with me.

Although we knew there was significant support for the Palestinian cause within the ranks of the Australian Labor Party, we did not have an indication of where Shadow Foreign Affairs Minister, Senator Penny Wong, stood. She is a formidable intellect and a highly valued member of the ALP front bench but seemingly cautious on this issue. In late October she was hosted by Federal Victorian Labor MP Peter Khalil at an event at the Thunder Road Brewery. It was to be a Q and A discussion 'on foreign aid, foreign policy and Australia's place in the world'. Tickets sold fast and I was unable to procure one. I wanted to ask her about her thoughts on recognition of Palestine. That opportunity would have to wait. However, I was able to watch a video of proceedings. Senator Wong was impressive. She said that on foreign policy 'the difference between the Liberal Party and the Labor Party was that although both dealt with the world the way it is, Labor sought to change it for the better'. I liked that Senator Wong, ever the cool pragmatist, had neatly articulated a policy framework difference that distinguished Labor from the Coalition. Within that broad context there surely must be room to make some 'change for the better' in regard to the Palestinian question. Some hope was raised in my mind as we got down to last minute details on our project.

The old routine of training walks of increasing distance and frequency was well underway. We would be on track for the departure date of 20 November. Feet and legs were as well conditioned to the rigours of the 737 kilometre walk as they would ever be. The decals displaying the *raison d'etre* of the project were pasted onto the support vehicle.

Jessica Morrison suggested that we change the date of departure from 20 to 18 November. The reason being that the annual Run for Palestine was being held on 18 November. It would be great to begin the walk with a gathering of supporters, in one place, at the Melbourne Botanical Gardens. Serendipitous but difficult to organise as all our accommodation was already booked. In the end we decided to compromise and begin on the Sunday, have a couple of days off, then resume on 21 November.

There is little point in doing long range walks for a cause if you do not attempt to spread the word. I had some assistance in these matters. I wrote a press release which was distributed by Sara Saleh, an employee of APAN. She also advised on the best format to use on social media. We set up a Cause Page on Facebook, entitled John Walks for Palestine 2018. I sent out a series of emails to Labor MPs and Senators who I was aware were not anti-Palestinian. I mentioned the walk to Adelaide and the motivation behind it. We also asked that, if convenient, they say hello to us in Adelaide at the completion of the walk.

2018 Walk from Melbourne to Adelaide

Day 1 – Melbourne to Caroline Springs: 18 November 2018

On Sunday 18 November we gathered at the Melbourne Botanical Gardens in Linlithgow Avenue. It was the annual occasion of the Run for Palestine. It was a perfect warm, sunny day. I was especially pleased to be joined by three men for the first day of the project: Nasser Mashni, Shane McCartin and Mark Bradbeer. Nasser Mashni is of Palestinian descent, though born in Australia. He is, naturally enough, a committed supporter of justice for Palestine. He is also the Treasurer of APAN. Shane and Mark are simply two Anglo-Celtic origin men who, like me, feel the treatment of the Palestinians by Australian governments has been woeful and needs to change. All three were fantastic walking companions through the back streets of Footscray, Sunshine and Deer Park. I enjoyed listening to many tales of their advocacy and activism for the Palestinian cause over the years. There is strength in solidarity. We stopped for lunch at a shopping centre in Sunshine.

Strangely enough, walking out of a major city like Melbourne is a little complicated because walking on freeways is not only dangerous but prohibited. Our journey contained a few doglegs and detours. We arrived at Caroline Springs to a lovely welcome. Jessica Morrison had organised a dinner by the lake and the local

Palestinian community were out in force to wish us well. Caroline Springs itself turned out to be clean, green and organised to a surprising extent. The four of us had a quiet beer and reflected on our day's work. Much more to come for me but at least we were en route at last. Nasser organised a taxi back to Melbourne for us. I was back at home by 9.30 pm. Meanwhile, the Facebook page – John Walks for Palestine 2018 – was attracting quite a lot of interest.

Day 2 – Caroline Springs to Bacchus Marsh: 21 November 2018

After two days furlough, the project resumed on 21 November. I was up at 4.30 am and drove to Caroline Springs Railway Station. I parked the car there and began walking on the back roads to Bacchus Marsh. Unlike day one, it was a solitary slog along fairly deserted roads. Greigs Road and Exford Road are back roads in Bacchus Marsh. Most of us would take the Western Freeway (M8) if driving. There was very little commercial activity but I had packed my own provisions. In this instance the back roads added a kilometre or two to the journey. I arrived at Bacchus Marsh Railway Station before 3 pm. I was weary, but like on Sunday, feeling some real relief that the project had at long last begun. As in previous years, the thought of a little chunk of the whole being 'under one's belt' was satisfying.

The V-Line train carried me back to Caroline Springs and from there I drove home to East Malvern. I learnt that some members of the NSW Liberal Party want to expel former Prime Minister Malcolm Turnbull from their party. I also heard that President Trump is adamant that Saudi Prince Mohamed bin Salman will not be punished for the brutal murder of Jamal Khashoggi inside the Saudi Embassy. What a wonderful world we live in.

Day 3 – Bacchus Marsh to Ballan: 22 November 2018

The previous night was to be our last night at home for many weeks. My wife, Wendy, worked diligently to organise and pack everything we needed for the journey. Every conceivable requirement in terms of clothes and equipment was loaded into our SUV. Our little dog, Boston, sensed something was afoot with so much activity going on around her. She was possibly relieved when she learnt that she would not be staying home without us. We left at 9 am and arrived in Bacchus Marsh via the M8 Freeway by 10.30 am. I was getting into the habit of taking our supporters 'with us' on the trip by making regular live video postings on Facebook. A nice amount of interest was being shown in our endeavours. It was almost an adventure because we had to get involved physically and it was all into territory we were unfamiliar with.

As the previous day, this day was a quiet, back roads affair. Wendy stayed in Bacchus Marsh for a while, and then caught up with me around 1 pm, bringing lunch. By 4 pm the 24-kilometre walk had been completed. We drove on 39 kilometres to Ballarat. We had booked two nights' accommodation in this large rural city. Our upstairs apartment was large and modern. The owner, Marty, was not around, but he had left adequate instructions for our stay.

The weather was cool and we felt fine. Directly across from the bed and breakfast apartment was the office of Catherine King. She was the Opposition Health Minister and MP for the seat of Ballarat. I had sent her emails some weeks ago that had not been responded to. We took the opportunity to call in on her personally. Ms King's staff advised us that her office did not receive my emails due to a mishap with the email address on my part. Over the 48 hours we were there, we tried to make personal contact, but the local member was busy campaigning for local Labor candidates in the Victorian State Election.

We sent her another, correctly addressed, email with details of our project and asked if she would like to interact with us upon our arrival in Adelaide. A week or so after leaving Ballarat, we received a reply from her. She afforded us what I refer to as a 'proforma' reply. Polite, and mentioning, like Foreign Minister Julie Bishop did, Labor's desire for a two-state solution. However, she would not be able to say hello to us once we arrived in Adelaide due to her being too busy. I wondered if the distance to be walked was not of sufficient length for her.

Day 4 – Ballan to Ballarat: 23 November 2018

As we set off to begin the walk, I reflected on the interaction with Ballarat MP Catherine King. I always think it is useful to engage with MPs and Senators. As long as there is no unpleasantness involved. Being annoying is being painful. If you are annoying, you are probably doing more harm than good. However, the pro-Israel crowd hector, badger and involve themselves with those in power endlessly and effectively. If another perspective is not offered, how are our elected representatives supposed to think and respond?

The following day was a walk of 39 kilometres. My wife drove me back to Ballan. She stayed close by me in the car most of the day, keeping me well nourished and ensuring my spirits were kept up. It was very tough going due to the inclement weather. A note in my diary reads, 'Beethoven's 2nd of 4th kept my spirits up.' The 19th century maestro can be enjoyed via iPhone and earplugs. It is inspirational and uplifting music of the highest order.

I walked for almost nine hours. I was soaked through from persistent rain. My hands were so cold and numb that I could not unzip my clothes. My wife had gone on ahead and put on the electric log fire in the Lydiard Street apartment. It was a great relief to finally cover the distance and have a hot shower. That evening we went out for dinner to another fashionable eatery in Ballarat. Over dinner we spoke of the Victorian State Election the next day.

Whatever differences the two major parties had, on one issue they were united: support for Israel. Whether it was Dan Andrews or Matthew Guy, no difference was discernible. Nonetheless, it was influencing politicians at the federal level that was most important for our cause. That is where foreign policy is made. That was where our advocacy must be directed.

Day 5 – Ballarat to Lake Burrumbeet: 24 November 2018

After the previous day's very testing conditions, we planned for only a very shortish walk this day. I was to walk from Ballarat to Lake Burrumbeet Caravan Park and it was only 18 kilometres. The Ballarat Avenue of Honour begins with a large arch on the outskirts of the city. From that arch onwards, every step of our journey that day was in the Avenue of Honour. That was because, amazingly, it is 22 kilometres long, and stretches way out past our overnight destination at Lake Burrumbeet Caravan Park. The path is lined with thousands of trees, each one dedicated to a serviceman from the Ballarat area who participated in World War I. It is unique, humbling and impressive. It is also a reminder of the tragedy of so many young Australian men dying in faraway places.

We had lunch near Cardigan. Once we arrived at Lake Burrumbeet, I felt good enough to keep walking for an hour or two and then subtract the distance from the next day's walk. This was to become a useful aspect of this trip, a luxury that was never available to me on previous Sydney to Canberra walks. On this trip I could simply walk until I was too tired, then call my wife who would come and pick me up. Then the following day I could simply resume the walk where my wife picked me up the day before.

That evening our accommodation was the opposite of our semi-luxurious apartment of the previous two nights. Caravan park cabins are family holiday style set-ups. We did, however, have a television, so we were able to watch the live results of the Victorian State Election. It was early in the night when analysts predicted that Matthew Guy and the Liberal Party were going to be vanquished by the government of Premier Dan Andrews and the Labor Party.

Day 6 – Lake Burrumbeet to Beaufort: 25 November 2018

Even though it was late November, it was quite cold in Lake Burrumbeet. The morning after analysis by media outlets and assorted commentators on the large State Labor Party win was fascinating. Was any of it attributable to the turmoil going on in the Federal Coalition government? In other words, was the defeat of the Coalition at next year's federal poll inevitable? From the perspective of Palestine, that would be positive. The Liberal and National parties in Australia are far less likely to be interested in issues of global injustice. Palestine is a prime example. If a political party is unconcerned about the concentration of wealth at the top end of society, then almost certainly that party will be less progressive on social issues and more relaxed about injustice in international affairs. It is the same in America and the UK. There are notable exceptions, however, like Malcolm Fraser and Peter Baume from the Liberal Party of yesteryear.

Shane McCartin advised me by email that he would pound the pavement for Palestine with me again today. True to his word, his car pulled into the caravan park at 8 am. Wendy drove us to the walk resumption point. By now the main highway to Adelaide was no longer a pedestrian free zone. It was still quite a cool day. Shane and I completed the 20 kilometres by noon. After a roadside lunch organised by Wendy, we decided to walk on a further 11 kilometres from Beaufort towards Ararat. After being picked up by Wendy, I drove Shane back to his car at Lake Burrumbeet and said farewell to him. The world is the better for people like him. We were so fortunate to have his company and support today.

Back at Beaufort my wife settled us in at the Beaufort Motel. It was a little precarious with the canine member of the family, as a prominent sign in our room said dogs were 'not allowed' but we hung a towel over the sign and ensured she was very quiet. We had dinner at the local pub. It was the first meal of many such meals in many such pubs.

Day 7 – Beaufort to Ararat: 26 November 2018

I learnt something recently about a much earlier activist who walked to protest the abuse of human rights. This was in 1938 by Aboriginal man William Cooper. He walked 10 km from his home in Footscray to Melbourne's CBD where he delivered a petition to the German consulate. Flanked by his family, friends, and members of the Australian Aboriginal League, the petition he presented said,

'On behalf of the Aboriginal inhabitants of Australia, we wish to have it registered and on record that we protest wholeheartedly at the cruel persecution of the Jewish people by the Nazi government in Germany. We plead that you would make it known to your government and its military leaders that this cruel persecution of their fellow citizens must be brought to an end.'

William Cooper was rebuffed by the German Consul General in Melbourne, unsurprisingly. In June 2018 the Australian Electoral Commission changed the federal Division of Batman to the Division of Cooper in his honour.

Shane and I had wiped 11 kilometres off the 43 kilometres between these two towns the previous day. Of the remaining 34 kilometres, there was little to report. It was flat and uninteresting terrain with just the unending horizon ahead of me. It became hot at the end of the day. There were loads of flies as well. Two Melbourne friends aware of the project met us as they travelled back to Melbourne from Adelaide. That was a very pleasant diversion for the day. Thank you, Kevin and Margaret Mitchell. The town of Ararat showed off a proud history going back to the early days of European colonisation. We had dinner at the RSL Club. Our accommodation was at a very comfortable bed and breakfast.

Day 8 – Ararat to Stawell: 27 November 2018

This day marked the eighth day of our project. I had a few little blisters and minor leg issues, but we were very happy with the progress we had made so far. I had my wife looking after me, so perhaps I shouldn't have been surprised. We had breakfast and I made a phone call or two before heading out to Stawell. I walked a distance of 30 kilometres that day. My wife brought lunch to me around midday just outside the tiny town of Great Western. We reached Stawell by 4.30 pm. We had another slightly precarious accommodation concern as we stayed in a motel that forbade dogs. We smuggled her into the room under the cover of darkness. Stawell is known for the Stawell Gift, Australia's most famous short distance running race, held there every Easter.

That evening we learnt of some quite amazing developments in the Federal Liberal Party. Julia Banks, MP for the Victorian seat of Chisolm, would quit the Coalition and move to the crossbench. Among the reasons for her decision: unequal treatment of women and the navel gazing of the 'reactionary and regressive right wing' of the Liberal Party. Along with the decision of Julie Bishop to move to the backbench, Julia Banks' decision revealed serious fissures within the federal parliamentary Liberal Party ranks.

Day 9 – Stawell to Dadswells Bridge: 28 November 2018

Overnight in Stawell we noticed that our Pomeranian dog Boston's left eye had completely closed over and the area around it had swelled significantly. She would not let us touch it as it was so painful.

The Stawell Veterinary Clinic allayed our concerns somewhat by advising it was a grass seed that had become embedded in her eye. Removal was relatively straightforward but she would need a general anaesthetic and 4–5 hours in their care. I began the day's walk to Dadswells Bridge, leaving Wendy in Stawell with Boston. I was most relieved to see both of them meet me for lunch at 1 pm. Her eye was by then partially open already and improved quickly over the next couple of days.

That day was another hot and tiring day pounding the pavement for Palestine. 30 kilometres would have been enough, however it ended up being 34 kilometres as our overnight accommodation was 4 kilometres west of the Dadswells Bridge township. We stayed that evening at the Orchid Lane Cottages which were clean and well equipped. Our host even provided me with a bottle of his own home brew beer. He must have noticed my condition! There was nowhere to eat much in the tiny town of Dadswells Bridge so we drove 30 kilometres into Horsham for dinner.

The Facebook page dedicated to our project was growing quickly. We were flattered with the attention the cause was receiving.

The Victorian Liberal Party leader, Matthew Guy, also resigned that day. Aside from his (mostly) unappealing policy prescriptions for the State of Victoria he was an unabashed boots-and-all fan of Israel. That was a common infection in the Australian political ferment.

Day 10 – Dadswells Bridge to Horsham: 29 November 2018

We had a very pleasant overnight stay at Orchid Lane Cottages. Our host was friendly and we slept peacefully. We were almost sad to leave. The cottages were a kilometre or two off the Western Highway and a short drive by my wife returned me to the bitumen for another day. She met up with me at Green Lake with a prepared lunch. Thereafter the trudge towards Horsham resumed. Horsham is a major rural Victorian city and was reached by 3 pm.

Our accommodation in Horsham was on a farming property on the Wimmera River. It was a self-contained building adjacent to Graham and Buffy's farmhouse. 'The Shack' was a unique and amazing retreat. We were going to be there for two nights. Our hosts had some sympathy for the Palestinian cause. It is fair to say that people we met, out there in the countryside, were quite astonished at our commitment to undertake such an endeavour, and for a cause with which we had no direct relation ourselves. On the other hand, it may enhance the impact. Over the course of almost four weeks we encountered mildly dissenting voices only twice. Overwhelmingly we found that if people had an interest in the issue, it was with a positive attitude towards the Palestinian cause.

It was great to have a variety of dining options in Horsham. The city was clean and well managed from all accounts. By this time, it was almost the end of November. The Prime Minister, Scott Morrison, had still not announced the government's decision on whether or not to move Australia's embassy from Tel Aviv to Jerusalem.

Day 11 – Horsham to Dimboola: 30 November 2018

When planning for this trip back in Melbourne, we had slotted in a couple of days of rest. Today was such a day. However, I decided to keep walking for three reasons: I was feeling pretty good; I wanted to build up a buffer of kilometres in case they were needed in the days ahead; and the next day was going to be rather hot. I started at 7.30 am and had completed 18 kilometres by 11.30 am. My wife picked me up and returned me to Horsham and the Shack, where we rested for the afternoon. The farming property we were staying at had four dogs. Those four dogs attacked our tiny dog that afternoon. I had to quickly intervene and save her from serious injury. It was very nasty and traumatic for our 3.5 kilogram Pomeranian. Buffy, our bed and breakfast host, thought her four dogs may have mistaken our dog for a rabbit or a cat. An unpleasant incident but not the fault of our hosts.

As always, I spent time each day updating the Walk's Facebook page. Little videos taken with an iPhone were uploaded to keep our supporters *au fait* with our progress. Many responses were received from people all over Australia and around the world. We returned to the city for dinner at the Horsham Community Club.

Day 12 – Horsham to Dimboola: 1 December 2018

I finished off the remaining 16 kilometres to Dimboola by 11.30 am. My wife walked with me for a short part of the distance. The temperature was in the mid-thirties by midday. We were unable to check into our bed and breakfast in Dimboola until 4 pm so returned to Horsham to attend an art and craft fair. Horsham is everything Dimboola is not: prosperous and displaying strong city pride. Poor old Dimboola is a sleepy town with little to recommend it. However, we had a reasonably good country pub dinner at the Victoria Hotel. It was virtually the only place serving dinner in Dimboola.

Day 13 – Dimboola to Nhill: 2 December 2018

As much as our journey was long and gruelling, it was not as epic as the trek of a certain Swedish man by the name of Benjamin Ladraa. He walked from Sweden to Palestine with the aim of informing the world about the situation of Palestine and spread awareness about the Israeli military occupation. His walk took place over 10 months, from August 2017 to June 2018, and he passed through 13 countries! Bravo Benjamin.

Staying in Dimboola had not been easy. Our host Barbara was pleasant but the facilities were basic. Our dog Boston was having epileptic fits, despite being on medication prescribed to alleviate this condition. Our veterinary surgeon suggested the trauma of the dog attack in Horsham might be causing the fits. We continued with her normal medication and she soon improved.

We had planned to walk only 17 kilometres this day but, once again, abandoned the plan and walked 36 kilometres. It was cool weatherwise and I felt up to a long day out there on the pavement.

We had begun to use Twitter as well as Facebook to advertise and promote the walk. There were some very positive and interesting responses from faraway places. There were little acts of solidarity with the Palestinian cause going on all over the world. You could see them on social media constantly, a bit like there used to be against South Africa back in the days of apartheid. The advent of social media just makes the cross-pollination between activists so much easier. Israeli trolls and professional propagandists are, by necessity, rather busy attempting to put out scrub fires all over the place. How they must long for an end to it all. Unfortunately for them, it is unlikely that the world will ever accept the suffering of the Palestinians as a *fait accompli*. Subjugation and inequality don't look like long-term bets for treatment of fellow human beings.

We stayed in Dimboola a second night as per our booking. The only Dimboola eating establishment, the Victoria Hotel, was closed on Mondays. Therefore we had to drive back into Horsham for dinner. It was at least 60 kilometres from where the day's walk ended.

Day 14 – Nhill to Kaniva: 3 December 2018

President George HW Bush had died the previous day, aged 94. One is tempted to look back with something like a modicum of approval for the 'old days'. President No. 41 was undoubtedly more sane and better informed than the current occupant of the White House. But in challenging Israel's behaviour against the indigenous people of Palestine, as this writer is doing, one might ask, is it any different to numerous American presidents of yesteryear who trampled on the rights of the indigenous tribes of America? In truth, it is difficult to look back and approve the actions of presidents from George Washington onwards with regard to the relentless expansion of settlers westward over native American land. The issue of Palestine raises these issues elsewhere, at least historically. Australia is no different.

Our stay in Dimboola had not been easy and we were almost relieved to be on the road again early that morning. We drove back to Nhill and walked 30 kilometres towards Kaniva. For many days we had been walking in wheat growing lands. The fertile plains spread out on either side of the road as far as the eye could see. Occasionally we saw the wheat being harvested, a phenomenally efficient operation with little manpower required. Case IH or John Deere harvesting machines do what hundreds of manual labourers must have done in years gone by. My wife brought me lunch out on the road as always. The sight of the vehicle approaching around midday was bliss. Victuals have never been more appreciated or so ravenously devoured. Our bed and breakfast at Nhill that evening was wonderful. Our host at 'Wendy's Retreat' even cooked dinner for us. I reflected, that evening, that being out on the road was not always all bad. It even felt like an adventure sometimes.

Day 15 – Kaniva to Bordertown: 4 December 2018

Wendy and her husband Darryl were great country folk. They made us a lavish breakfast before we hit the road. Of interest were the stories they told us of how well the Karen people of Burma had integrated into the community of Nhill. They had arrived here as refugees over the past ten years and now make up nearly 20% of the town's workforce. From all accounts, a wonderful success story as they integrate into the Nhill community.

We were wearing jackets early that morning. The feet were not troubling me much despite being subjected to hundreds of kilometres of pavement pounding. I applied a good coating of Vaseline to them each morning. We reached Kaniva at lunchtime and kept going during the afternoon. Another 30 kilometres were completed that day. Jessica Morrison phoned me to advise that AFOPA (Australian Friends of Palestine Association) were conscious of our efforts and would leverage our arrival on 16 December to promote recognition initiatives at the Labor Party Conference in Adelaide.

Day 16 – Kaniva to Bordertown: 5 December 2018

We were on the road at 7.15 am, thanks to the efforts of my wonderfully supportive wife. There were pleasant enough perambulations before the heat set in. I managed to get on the Jon Faine ABC Melbourne radio programme talkback session at 10.45 am. We managed to convey some aspects of our project to his many Melbourne listeners. The temperature got to 35 degrees Celsius at around 1.30 pm. At that time, we were safely ensconced in the air-conditioned comfort of the support vehicle. We had arranged two nights' stay in Bordertown at a self-contained unit in Golf Course Road. We had no contact with the hosts but were in a very well equipped place with terrific facilities. We had dinner at the Woolshed Inn, which was only a stone's throw away from a statue of former Prime Minister Bob Hawke. He was born in Bordertown and the town likes to advertise that fact. It was worth noting again that, along with other former ALP luminaries, he was in favour of Australia recognising Palestine.

Another milestone was achieved today. We were now in South Australia. Kaniva was the last significant town in Victoria. There was no sign announcing where the two states converged out there on the Western Highway A8.

Day 17 – Bordertown to Keith: 6 December 2018

There was a distance of 47 kilometres between these two towns but we were going to forego a planned day of rest the next day and walk two days of 23 or so kilometres. It was entirely sensible because the forecast temperatures were in the mid-thirties. My wife had me out walking by 6 am. The temperature was great at that hour, but no matter what hour one walked at, it was just relentlessly dry and flat terrain. To keep my sanity, I listened to the radio via the ubiquitous iPhone and a set of earplugs – ABC Radio National Breakfast with Fran Kelly from 6 am, switching to ABC Melbourne with Jon Faine at 8.30 am. By 11 am we were finished for another day. The sun does not have a chance to impact the solitary perambulator too much by that time. However, 50+ sunscreen was liberally applied to the body each day. Just before I was picked up by my wife, a South Australian Highway Patrol car pulled up alongside me. The two officers on board were only desirous of my welfare, offering me a bottle of cold water. They were great guys who even expressed some sympathy with the Palestinian cause.

Back in Bordertown that afternoon I watched the final Question Time from Parliament House in Canberra. Those days were grim for the Coalition. The voting public had been given no credible explanation for the ousting of former Prime Minister Malcolm Turnbull. Sitting female MPs had repeatedly expressed misgivings about the bullying and intimidation by sections of the Liberal Party towards them. Polls indicated the chances of the Coalition winning the next election were modest. The issue of Palestine was hardly front and centre in the minds of the voting public, neither should it be. However, the chances of Labor winning in May 2019 were high, and they were much more sympathetic to the cause than the Coalition. I could not but be pleased at the direction in which things were moving.

Day 18 – Bordertown to Keith: 7 December 2018

Our second day en route to Keith was forecast to be even worse than day one, in terms of searing heat. Therefore, my wife had me up even earlier than the day before – arising at 4 am, followed by walking at

5 am. At this rate she would soon have me up even before I went to bed from the day before!

It was Friday and I was sure that as usual, it being Friday, there would be hundreds if not thousands of Gaza Palestinians protesting near the fence that Israel had erected to enclose them (let's restate that Israel does not consider this to be a border). It was certain that some of those young people would not come home tonight. It was certain that some wretched parent, wife, brother or sister would mourn a loved one cut down in their prime. It was also probably certain that the Israeli snipers who pulled the triggers on the weapons that would kill those unarmed protesters would do so without troubling their consciences (as they had become so blinded by an ideology that espouses extreme tribalism). When I thought of such brutality, and conversely such bravery and determination, it was strong motivation for me to keep walking no matter what the temperature. Weariness and sore legs and feet are the, somewhat pitiful, sole consequences of this and other projects. I am safe. I am free. Is it too much to ask for the same for Palestinians?

The heat must have slowed me somewhat as the 23 kilometres took me until 11 am to complete. Back in Bordertown we made a short video about the day's events in front of the statue of Bob Hawke. We then uploaded the video to various social media platforms as usual. After that we returned to our Bordertown bed and breakfast, packed up and drove to Keith. Our hosts at the new bed and breakfast in Keith were genuine country folks. Brett was a wool buyer and his wife Renae was a shearer. We had yet another country pub meal that evening. It had been up to 41 degrees Celsius today. Cold beer never tasted better. The next day was forecast to be cooler, thankfully.

Day 19 – Keith to Tintinara: 8 December 2018

By now any concept of walking to a destination in a day had become redundant. I just walked until I could walk no more and I would then call the cavalry to come and pick me up. The next day I would just resume the walk from that pick-up point. The temperature was only 22 degrees. We walked 25 kilometres and could perhaps have done more. I was so fortunate to have my wife with me. I can never say that enough. The love of my life and the most wonderful company, especially when I know I annoy the hell out of her at times. That afternoon we relaxed at Keith, watching the Test Cricket being played in Adelaide. Brett and Renae were away fishing. We had another basic fare dinner at the Keith Hotel.

I read that Nikki Haley was disgracing and embarrassing herself even further as a craven shill for Israel. Her final act as US Ambassador to the UN was to put a resolution to the UN General Assembly condemning Hamas. The resolution failed. Haley had resigned her post, unlike so many others who were fired by President Trump. Today, for example, Chief of Staff General John Kelly was fired. Nikki Haley will no doubt return as a Republican candidate for the Oval Office in years to come. Her pro-Israel credentials are just too strong to believe we have seen the last of her.

Day 20 – Keith to Tintinara: 9 December 2018

This morning Wendy walked with me for a kilometre or two. She continued to have severe back issues but did enjoy walking. As usual we were out on the road as the sun rose. I completed 30 kilometres. I walked past the tiny town of Tintinara for a few kilometres. Like in most towns out there, a large grain elevator was prominent. We stayed overnight at O'Deas Cottage. It was a self-contained residence on a farm owned by a young farming family. My wife was horrified when I advised her that I saw a large snake slither past the building that afternoon. Our dog Boston was immediately confined indoors for the remainder of our stay.

Day 21 – Tintinara to Coonalpyn: 10 December 2018

Lying in bed in the early hours of the morning at O'Deas Cottage, we realised that there was only one week left of this sojourn. By then we would have arrived in Adelaide. That realisation put a little spring in my step. We contemplated staying another night at the cottage. It was spacious and comfortable and the owners offered it to us for a second night. In the end we decided to take a risk and move on to the dubious delights of the Coonalpyn Hotel, where we had made a booking.

Another day, another early start, another 30 kilometres. I kept my mind firmly on the goal and used music to relieve the boredom. Beethoven was a gift to the world that keeps on giving. We checked into the Coonalpyn Hotel around 4 pm. I sent off some emails to various MPs and Senators. I made a few phone calls as well. One only speaks to office staff, of course, but even engaging with them has some usefulness. The excitement of finishing our project stimulated me to attempt this interaction, even though I was invariably very tired.

We rather liked the Coonalpyn Hotel. It was a true bush pub in that you quickly get to know the publican. Such pubs take on institutional status at times in small towns. I was reminded of pubs in Marulan and Tarago which have a similar charm. Also, for the weary and hungry itinerants, they are one stop shops. You only have to wander down the corridor to reach the bar or the dining room. Hearty meals are even prepared with some love and care here. The publican is always good for a chat. It is part of his job! You leave a little bit of yourself behind in such places, in spite of it being basic and slightly rough. If ever we are back this way again we would surely call in for at least a drink.

Day 22/23 – Coonalpyn to Tailem Bend: 11 and 12 December 2018

This journey took two days. It was a distance of about 67 kilometres. Day one saw us having lunch at the tiny town of Ki Ki. A park there was dedicated to old machinery used in the local wheat harvest. After completing the 30 or so kilometres, we drove into Tailem Bend for an hour or so until we checked into the bed and breakfast where we would spend the next two nights. We were staying in Wellington East Marina. Our delightful hosts were great company. We were recommended the Wellington Hotel for dinner. It was across the Murray River, with access via a free car ferry (free because it is part of the National Highway). Unique.

We received some discouraging news that day. Firstly, we were advised that Shadow Foreign Affairs Minister Penny Wong would not have time to say hello to us at the Adelaide Conference Centre. Secondly, we heard that the Australian government had decided to move the Australian Embassy to Jerusalem. The source of this rumour was reliable, but the next morning we could find no confirmation of it in serious media outlets. We found out a couple of days later that the embassy would not be moved.

Day two saw us drive out on the Dukes Highway for 20 kilometres eastwards so we could resume from the point we stopped at the day before. For some reason it was the worst thing to do – drive the distance you know you are about to walk. It always feels like a huge distance. Wendy walked a kilometre with me before returning to the car. We took the opportunity to make another video for our Facebook project page. Once uploaded, it reached 6300 people. I walked through the town of Tailem Bend and on towards Murray Bridge for 7 more kilometres. When Wendy picked me up at 12.30 pm, I was almost melting, such was the heat.

That evening, Anne and Bruce cooked us a three course dinner at the Wellington East Marina. It was very pleasant but I was unable to cool down after being out in the sun at midday, no matter how many litres of cold fluid I drank.

Day 24 – Tailem Bend to Murray Bridge and beyond: 13 December 2018

One has plenty of time to think whilst pounding the pavement for Palestine. One has to keep one's wits in place too...constantly avoiding the backdraught of semi-trailers that whoosh by. Today I thought back to the days of 1990 when Nelson Mandela was released from prison. He served 27 years behind bars for demanding equal rights. I vividly recall the joyous scenes in South Africa when freedom finally came. Despite predictions of reprisals and a bloodbath, it did not happen.

East Timor, too, finally secured freedom in 2002 after years of struggle against Indonesian occupation.

We can equally imagine that wonderful, joyous day when Palestine achieves freedom. Whether it be by a two-state or one-state solution.

If the previous day was unbearably hot, this day was the opposite. It was only an 18-kilometre walk to Murray Bridge today, but I barely made it. By the time I walked across the lovely old bridge to enter the city of Murray Bridge, I was wet through and the umbrella mangled by the severe winds that blew that morning. I hoped that following lunch at the Bridgeport Hotel we would be able to do a few more miles, but the rain intensified.

That evening we stayed at yet another unique and charming bed and breakfast in Murray Bridge, from where we made more calls to Labor politicians, advising them of our project and that we would love to engage with them at the Adelaide Conference Centre. What we noticed was that to some extent our work was just a back-up to the work done by APAN already. Whilst it surely is easy to take the side of the bullied and oppressed, in the case of Palestine it is also challenging because the pro-Israel lobby advocates are so practised in the art of deception and dissembling. There appears to be a groundswell of members of the Labor Party who see this as an issue that progress must be made on. After discussions with my friends at APAN, I felt hopeful about what would happen in Adelaide on the weekend.

Whilst the rain was impeding our progress in South Australia, there was sunshine in Perth where the 2nd Cricket Test was being played. Australia was doing a little better this time, although India was the dominant team.

Day 25 – Murray Bridge to Callington: 14 December 2018

On yesterday's walk I reflected on Nelson Mandela's release from prison in 1990. Being a man of principle, he was not backward in coming forward on the issue of Palestine. As has already been mentioned in these pages, he considered freedom for Palestinians as unfinished business. Whilst Mandela was in prison for the 1970s and 1980s, apartheid-era South Africa and Israel formed close military ties.

When Mandela died in 2013, virtually every world leader attended his funeral. The leaders of Israel were conspicuous by their absence. Both President Peres and Prime Minister Netanyahu excused themselves for unconvincing reasons.

For a detailed and shocking history of the collaboration between apartheid-era South Africa and Israel, read *The Unspoken Alliance* by Sasha Polakow-Suransky.

The next morning we had to wait until the rain stopped before perambulating again. We resumed from the Bridgeport Hotel on towards Callington. I walked 14 kilometres before lunch and 12 kilometres after lunch. We had to drive all the way to Aldgate for our overnight accommodation (it was the only available bed and breakfast in the area that accepted dogs). We had entered the Adelaide Hills area. There was an immediate contrast in topography after so many days in the wheat belts of the Wimmera. Dinner that evening was at the Stirling Hotel and it was different too, the antithesis of a country pub. It was swank and sophisticated as befits the affluent Adelaide Hills.

Day 26 – Callington to Hahndorf: 15 December 2018

We drove through the Hahndorf township the previous day and did so twice again on that day. That was because Aldgate was beyond Hahndorf. This morning we drove through it on the way to Callington where we resumed our walk. For the first time in many days we were forced to walk on back roads. That was because we were approaching Adelaide and the driving route went from being a highway to a (pedestrian prohibited) freeway. The shortest route was using the Back Callington Road. It was extremely remote, almost akin to a bush track. The 28 kilometres was tough going. I was really pleased to finally march into Hahndorf town to be met by my wonderful wife. After I showered at Aldgate, we drove back to Hahndorf to wander the very tourist orientated streets. Hahndorf was settled by German migrants in the 1830s and it retains its Germanic characteristics even now.

Being in Hahndorf raised the issue of modern day Germany's position on Palestine. It is not the right position for Germany to hold. What Germany did in the 1930s and 1940s was horrific and they have made sincere efforts to atone. One only has to visit Berlin to see public reminders of the sins of the past, for example, the Memorial to the Murdered Jews of Europe. In their atonement, however, they seem to think any criticism of Israel is completely off limits. In view of the appalling treatment of Palestinians by Israel, and Germany's complete refusal to speak up about it, a second injustice by Germany is being perpetrated. Being silent when another group

The team,
November
2018

About to load
the car

Leaving Ballarat

Over half the journey completed

The long and
(seldom)
winding road

Trekker's food

Do we have to?

Crossing into Murray Bridge

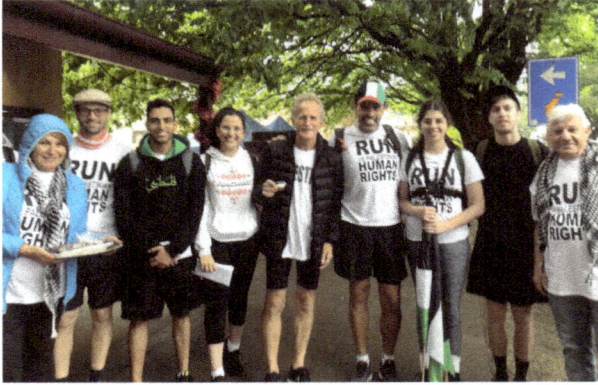

The last day, December 2018. About to depart Hahndorf.

Rundle Mall

Adelaide Convention Centre, 16 December 2018

of people is being discriminated against only compounds the earlier discrimination.

That evening we were recommended by our bed and breakfast host, Suzy, to have dinner at the Crafers Hotel a few kilometres up the road towards Adelaide. It was a rather upmarket and sophisticated venue compared to so many others we had visited. There was huge excitement ahead of tomorrow. Prior to beginning the project, we often spoke of the 'if' of making it all the way to Adelaide. Now there was no doubt.

Day 27 – Hahndorf to Adelaide: 16 December 2018

It is difficult to describe the satisfaction and relief that we felt on that day as we arrived in Adelaide. Exactly a month prior we had begun the walk from Melbourne's Botanical Gardens. Here is how the day unfolded.

As arranged with the indefatigable Nasser Mashni, we met up with him in Hahndorf that morning along with about 15 other supporters from Adelaide. There was much good humour and some outpourings of love and appreciation towards us, especially from those with a Palestinian background. Many joining the walk today were younger than me by a considerable margin and the pace was more brisk than usual. For large parts of the day we walked on bush paths. The support vehicle and Wendy could only keep in touch by phone. We reached 60 Frome Street as planned at 4 pm. That is the headquarters of AFOPA (Australian Friends of Palestine Association). A large crowd of further supporters welcomed us, and once Wendy got a car park, we all marched as a large throng through Rundle Mall and then to the Adelaide Convention Centre.

The entrance to the building is via a significant set of steps and then one has to turn left onto a walkway which takes you to the entrance. The last few dozen steps felt surreal, as we could see a large crowd of wellwishers. APAN, Wendy Turner and others had successfully promoted our project to delegates at the Labor conference. Palestinian flags were everywhere as well as signs with the message 'Recognise Palestine. It's Time' that were held aloft by many. Up to 20 Federal MPs and Senators were present as well as State Labor politicians and other conference delegates.

I was invited to speak for a few minutes and tried to explain why I felt it worthwhile for us to undertake such activism, despite our having no direct skin in the game. I mentioned the two Australian cave divers Craig Challen and Richard Harris. These two men rescued 12 Thai boys trapped in a cave in June 2018. They answered the call for help despite the boys being unknown to them. They answered the call for help despite them being neither Thai nor Buddhist. They answered the call for help because they knew there was no way to save the boys without international assistance. There were comparisons, I asserted, with the situation of the Palestinians. Without outside help, 4 million Palestinians were 'trapped in a cave' of sorts and it was up to us to try and remedy that. After all, President Barack Obama famously said, 'Let there be no doubt, the situation of the Palestinians is intolerable.' Trying to bring justice to the Palestinian situation is the cause of our times. In the recent past other calls for justice have been heard and answered in South Africa and East Timor. The calls for justice and equal treatment can have dramatically less power and resonance if exemptions are attempted. Palestine must be free.

I also wanted to show some appreciation. Firstly, to all those who supported the walk, either physically or via social media. Secondly, to the terrific work of APAN whose lobbying efforts got us to the point we are at today. Thirdly, to those in the Labor Party who were working within the policy framework for change on this issue. And lastly, to thank my wonderful wife for putting up with a thousand inconveniences over the past six months.

Chief Opposition Whip Chris Hayes (NSW) and Senator Anne Urquhart (Tasmania) both spoke as well. There was a great feeling of solidarity and determination by all in attendance. We could only now wait to see what transpired at the conference.

From there we gathered at the Adelaide home of Bassam Dally for a celebratory dinner. Dr Dally is a Professor of Mechanical Engineering at Adelaide University and also Vice President of APAN. About 30 people attended. We had a memorable evening of delicious food, wine and solidarity. APAN President Bishop George Browning spoke to us briefly about how far we had come in our efforts over the past five or so years. He also encouraged us to maintain our efforts. George had only recently returned from a visit to Palestine and outlined the very dire situation there.

Day 28 – Adelaide to Melbourne:17 December 2018

There is a feeling of satisfaction that one feels after completing a gruelling physical event. The feeling must be similar to having run a 42-kilometre marathon or having successfully climbed a mountain. We felt some of those feelings the day before. Our stay in Adelaide was very brief, as we left our bed and breakfast early on Monday morning and returned home to Melbourne. What had taken a month to walk took only a day to drive. Sitting there in the driver's seat as the tarmac stretched out ahead, I could hardly believe that I had covered all those kilometres by foot.

The Result

ON TUESDAY AFTERNOON WE LEARNT THAT AT THE conference held in Adelaide, the Labor Party had enshrined in policy a new position on Palestine. The resolution passed unanimously and was proposed by the Shadow Foreign Affairs Minister herself, Senator Penny Wong, then seconded by Manager of Opposition Business in the House of Representatives, Tony Burke. The full resolution is listed below.

SENATOR THE HON PENNY WONG LEADER OF THE OPPOSITION IN THE SENATE SHADOW MINISTER FOR FOREIGN AFFAIRS LABOR SENATOR FOR SOUTH AUSTRALIA SPEECH

18 December 2018

ISRAELI/PALESTINIAN RESOLUTION – ALP NATIONAL CONFERENCE – ADELAIDE

*** check against delivery ***

I move this motion – but the text is the work of many.

I want to acknowledge that the conflict between Israel and Palestine is an issue of great importance to many in our Party.

It is of great importance because Labor is a friend of Israel. I am a friend of Israel.

It is of great importance because Labor is a friend of the Palestinians. I am a friend of the Palestinians.

It is of great importance because we, in Labor, not only deal with the world as it is, we seek to change it for the better.

And so all who have come to this debate do so in the hope of contributing to peace and to a just and lasting resolution of the conflict between these two peoples.

I thank everyone for the manner in which they have engaged to propose this resolution – which I am confident reflects the collective view of this conference.

This resolution makes clear the view of this conference is to continue to support the recognition and right of Israel and Palestine to exist as two states within secure and recognised borders.

And it recognises the desire of this conference to recognise Palestine as a state.

Labor has long supported, and continues to support, a two-state solution to the Israeli-Palestinian conflict.

We support Israel's right to exist within secure and recognised boundaries and the creation of a Palestinian state.

We recognise that a just two-state resolution will require recognising the right of both the Israeli and Palestinian peoples to live in peace and security.

The hallmark of Labor's approach has been our even-handedness, and our acceptance of the legitimate claims by both parties.

Labor has been consistent in its approach to working towards the resolution of conflict between Palestine and Israel.

We have been consistent in our criticism of actions that undermine progress.

The resort to violence or the use of disproportionate response.

The construction of new settlements in areas that will become part of a future Palestinian State and the retrospective legalisation of settlements.

Labor will continue to call on both sides of the conflict to refrain from any actions that hamper peaceful outcomes for both the Israeli and Palestinian people.

And we will continue to ensure that any decision we take contributes to peaceful resolution of the conflict and to progress towards a two-state solution.

It is an approach, which until recently, had been largely bipartisan.

But, in a shameful act five days before the Wentworth by-election, Scott Morrison put his own domestic political interest before the national interest.

He made a decision to junk longstanding bipartisan foreign policy in a cynical attempt to win votes.

It was a desperate political tactic.

It was a decision made against the longstanding advice of agencies, without Cabinet consideration, and without properly consulting Australia's partners and allies.

Astonishingly, it was a decision made without consulting either the Israelis or the Palestinians themselves, whose agreement must be the foundation of any lasting peace.

The result of the chaos and confusion has been clear.

Mr Morrison has caused offence to some of our nearest neighbours, harmed Australia's international reputation, and our nation's interests.

Ever since, the Prime Minister has been trying to escape the problem of his own creation.

It is a clear example of what happens when domestic politics is put before national interest.

Unlike Scott Morrison and his Government, Labor in Government will take a responsible approach to our foreign policy.

We will seek and consider the advice of our agencies.

We will work with our partners and allies.

We will always put the national interest first.

This motion makes clear Labor's commitment to progressing lasting peace and a two-state solution.

It makes clear that it will be an important priority for the next Labor Government.

As Labor's Shadow Minister for Foreign Affairs, I commend the resolution to the conference.

Authorised by Noah Carroll, ALP, Canberra.

For those of us seeking to progress the cause of Palestine justice, this was very heartening. Especially as polls consistently showed Labor would likely be the next government. I wrote another article for *Mondoweiss*.

MONDOWEISS

News & Opinion About Palestine, Israel & the United States

Australian Labor Party commits to recognizing Palestine

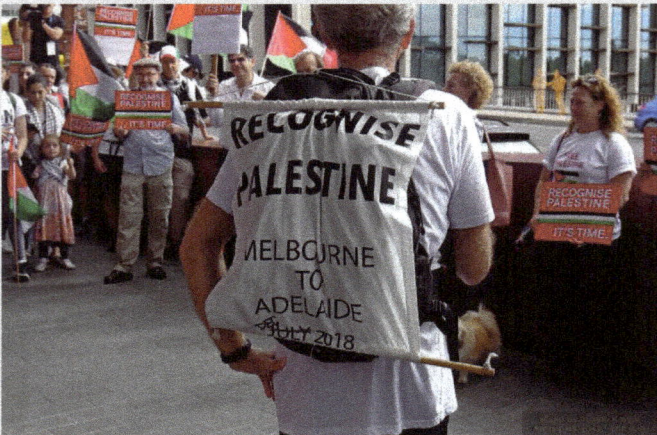

Labor supporters for the recognition of a Palestinian state, Adelaide, December 17, 2018. (Photo: APAN – Australia Palestine Advocacy Network/Facebook)

In Australia we have a significant lobbying force for the Palestinian position within the political sphere. The Australian Palestinian Advocacy Network (APAN) is quite active and effective at running campaigns to highlight the plight of Palestinians. For example, they have had great success with a campaign entitled "No Way to Treat a Child" which chronicled the conditions under which Palestinian children are convicted and incarcerated in military tribunals.

Along with elder statesman and former Foreign Minister Bob Carr, APAN has also been lobbying for recognition of the state of Palestine within the Australian Labor Party (ALP). The Labor Party is in opposition in the Australian parliament to the ruling center-right Coalition bloc, of Liberal and National party members.

Two weeks ago on December 16 to 18, the ALP held its triennial national conference in Adelaide, the capital of South Australia. Persistent efforts to engage with senior members of the current ALP parliamentary group appear to be having results. APAN is a very diverse group. On the executive board are a retired Anglican Bishop, Palestinians of both Muslim and Christian heritage, secularists and a professor of Jewish background. They all participated in efforts leading up to the conference as this is the arena where policy positions are debated and then adopted.

To attract further attention to the cause I undertook another long range advocacy walk to highlight the unequal treatment of Palestinians. From November 18 to December 16, the walk covered a distance of 458 miles (starting in Melbourne and finishing in Adelaide). Many MPs and Senators greeted our arrival in Adelaide. The arrival was specifically planned to coincide with the opening date of the ALP conference.

Bob Carr was overseas during the conference but made an address via video.

Delegates to the conference would also have been aware of support for recognition by former Prime Ministers Bob Hawke and Kevin Rudd and another long serving Foreign Minister, Gareth Evans.

There is still strong support for Israel within the ALP but those members who are fed up with continued settlement expansion have grown, and now outnumber those members who remain loyal to Israel "whatever it does".

On the final day of the conference, the new motion on Palestine was put forward by the Shadow Minister for Foreign Affairs Penny Wong. The motion was seconded by Tony Burke (a senior ALP figure who since entering Parliament in 2004 is the only member of the Federal Parliament to have always served as either a minister or shadow minister).

The resolution passed unanimously, albeit with an edit in the language substituting "immediate" recognition for an independent state of Palestine to a downgraded "important priority."

The breakthrough resolution commits the party to recognize Palestine. Timing of recognition will be decided by Cabinet, though it is described as an "important priority." Although this move by a future Australian government may be of little practical impact for the beleaguered Palestinians in their day to day struggle with their military occupation, the strategic implications are enormous for Israel. Will more nations follow Australia's move?

All this happens in the context of upcoming elections in May 2019 where opinion polls have consistently put Labor ahead of the center-right Liberal-National Coalition in a run-off. The latest news poll from December 7 shows a swing to Labor of 4.5 percent indicating they would win 89 of the 150 seats in Parliament.

How will Israel respond?

Australia has traditionally been one of the planet's most unequivocal supporters of everything Israel does. It often votes with the U.S. and Israel against motions condemning Israel at the United Nations, including being one of only six countries that voted no to a resolution put up by Ireland on December 7. Moreover, this month the government of Prime Minister Scott Morrison decided to recognize West Jerusalem as Israel's capital, though it will not move its embassy to Jerusalem.

Interesting days ahead.

John Salisbury

It was still not a *fait accompli*, however, that recognition of
Palestine by Australia would take place. That is because the pro-
Israel lobby would oppose it vigorously. It would be miraculous
if Bill Shorten found himself defending the move to recognise
Palestine by a future Australian government. He had never spoken
or acted in support of the Palestinian cause. For many years he had
been consistently supportive of Israel. He even led delegations to
Israel. The pressure on him to override or delay the Labor Party
resolution would be intense. The whole ethos of the Zionist
movement is inimical to the creation of a Palestinian state. The
only surprise would be if there were not huge efforts to prevent
the Australian Labor Party from recognising Palestine. That would
be the battleground, should Labor win the next federal election.
Nonetheless, real progress had been made. There were many people
to give credit for this: Bob Carr and Wendy Turner for prosecuting
the case within the Labor Party; the board and members of APAN
for their advocacy and commitment; the many Jewish organisations
in Australia who fight for Palestinian justice (e.g. the Australian
Jewish Democratic Society, Independent Jewish Voices Australia,
and Jews Against the Occupation Australia). Perhaps the most
credit should go to Israel itself. The relentless growth of settlements
in occupied territory had changed the mind of many about who was
responsible for the failure of a peaceful resolution of the situation.

The End of the Journey?

Many years and many kilometres ago my knowledge of the Palestine/Israel issue and Middle East peace was limited. I was not alone in my naivety. Leon Uris's famous novel informed our perception about Israel. It was always plucky little Israel defending itself against the overwhelming odds of murderous, unreasonable Muslim hordes. That is a gross distortion of history. In the 1940s and beyond, it was the Palestinians who were defending themselves against (mostly) European invaders.

Whatever the merits of the European Jews needing a safe place from European pogroms against them, it could never be right to inflict themselves so determinedly on the people who had lived on the land of Palestine for many centuries. What people would not have resisted when so much was taken away from them? It is hardly surprising that Palestinians called on friends in neighbouring countries to come to their assistance. The many books of Israeli historian Ilan Pappé detail the events comprehensively. That resistance continues today. Resistance against the wall, resistance against Jewish-only settlements that dot the West Bank, and resistance against the siege of Gaza.

I remember well hearing the call to do something tactile, something defining, to remedy the injustice, from Marcelo Svirsky back in 2014. Walking these journeys in Australia might seem a forlorn endeavour, an unlikely solution to an intractable problem occurring many thousands of kilometres away. Yet in a tiny way it might have been worthwhile. Could demanding equal treatment for a people who have been discriminated against ever be a worthless endeavour?

We do not know yet whether a future Labor government in Australia will make a step forward for justice and equality. Australia has long since recognised Israel. Successive Australian governments have stated they are firmly in favour of a two-state solution. So why not recognise the other state? In spite of making Palestinian recognition 'an important priority' via a resolution at the 2018 Labor Party Conference, we may see further prevarication as a result of intense lobbying and pressure from the pro-Israel lobby.

May 2019 Election Result

THE 18 MAY FEDERAL ELECTION RESULT DEFIED MONTHS OF poll results and saw the return of the LNP Coalition for a third term. Unlike the 25 July 2018 by-election results and the resounding victory of the marriage equality postal survey, the tide seemed to turn back to the Coalition under the leadership of the evangelical Christian Scott Morrison. Nobody would have been more surprised than those prominent Liberals who decided to end their political careers prior to the poll, Michael Keenan, Julie Bishop, Christopher Pyne and Kelly O'Dwyer. After all it has become a truism in Australia to say that 'disunity is death'.

A little part of me died that Saturday in May. Aside from the salient issues that Labor campaigned on, i.e. intergenerational equity; tax reform; climate change; a federal ICAC; Indigenous Peoples Treaty; adequate funding for the ABC etc., there was, for some of us, the issue of Palestinian recognition. It was deeply disappointing and depressing that Australia, for the next three years, would continue to ignore the 'intolerable situation' of the Palestinians. There is no reason why Coalition MPs could not have conservative positions on economic and social issues domestically, yet have some regard for persecuted people overseas. Except that they don't. With rare and notable exceptions (Sussan Ley, Craig Laundy, Mark Coulton), Coalition MPs are enthusiastically uncritical of Israel.

If Labor had won the election, then we could have expected, at some point during 2019–2022, that Australia would have formally recognised the State of Palestine. As a middle power, Australia joining the other 137 countries that recognise Palestine would have been a significant positive step. Now all hopes are dashed. It was a shattering blow for those of us seeking to promote the Palestinian cause.

Scott Morrison invoked a religious element to his election victory by saying he 'still believed in miracles'. There would be no miracles for Palestinians. In a sense there would be no more reliance on miracles for Israel either. Former President Shimon Peres may have said, 'There is no other truth but the truth of peace,' but he must have been joking. Israel believes in overwhelming military force and dealing with enemies by killing them first. That is the truth that Israel lives by.

Epilogue – Personal Reflections

MY GREAT-GRANDFATHER, JOHN PARK SALISBURY, ARRIVED IN Australia in 1852. The Salisbury family of Yorkshire lost the family fortune speculating on railroads, the dot-com bubble of that age. He left his career as an articled law clerk, aged 19, to seek to recover the family fortunes in Australia. His initial goal of farming was set aside temporarily to join countless others in gold prospecting. As that was unsuccessful, he became a pastoralist. I know his life story well because he wrote a fine book, *After Many Days*. It is my treasured possession. I include this here because he refers to the settler/colonialist aspect of his presence in Australia.

'The next day's march was past the Black Protectorate Director, who was commissioned by government to see that the tame blacks are not imposed upon, and to dole out to them stipends of flour sugar and blankets. A wise and kindly arrangement, seeing the white man has so overrun the black fellows' hunting grounds.'

My great-grandfather implicitly acknowledged the impact of strangers arriving in a land that was clearly not *terra nullius*. We know that there were many instances of slaughter of First Australians by immigrants from Great Britain. John Park Salisbury also spoke fondly of the Maoris he encountered in New Zealand. This is a personal relief to me as someone who is conscious of the impact of large numbers of people arriving by boat, uninvited, into lands where people are already well established.

A further reflection is from growing up in Wellington, New Zealand. In secondary school, a classmate, Mark Phillips, was the son of the South African Ambassador. His father, I remember, wrote numerous opinion pieces in local newspapers defending the iniquitous system of apartheid that was the policy of the white South African government.

I mention these two historical reflections in this book because they are relevant to the current situation in Palestine.

It is beyond dispute that Jews arriving as refugees from Europe did not arrive to find vacant land in Palestine. By the same measure, my great-grandfather could not deny he arrived in Australia to find that the land was not uninhabited. The migrants to Southern Africa from Holland and England, similarly encroached upon the native people of the land. In all instances, Palestine, Australia, New Zealand and South Africa, the indigenous inhabitants opposed European arrival and occupation.

We seldom reflect honestly on the colonial theft of First Nations sovereignty. In reality, there is no difference to the Aboriginal peoples protecting their land to our successful defence against the imminent invasion of the Japanese in 1944.

With the rise of the Third Reich in 1933, the Palestinians had to deal with a steady invasion of European Jewish folks. Like Australians, indigenous Palestinians tried to repel those wishing to take their land, but were unsuccessful. And yet Palestinians are criticised for attempting to hold on to what is theirs?

The difference in these three examples is Palestine. The other two issues have been sorted to the extent that ALL inhabitants of Australia and New Zealand enjoy democratic rights and freedoms, though inequities exist. Palestinians, however, live under a brutal military apartheid.

If one wonders why this appalling injustice has been allowed to linger and fester for over seven decades, in violation of numerous UN resolutions, then inevitably one comes back to the most powerful country on earth and the current unequivocal support they give to the tiny Middle East country. Why do they do so?

Two answers to that question stand out: 1. Money; and 2. Religion.

1. The American political system is awash with funds from various lobby groups such as the gun lobby, the pharmaceutical lobby, the Christian lobby and the Israel lobby. Just as Congressmen are too scared to vote in favour of gun reform because of the power of the NRA, they are scared to speak critically of Israel.

2. America is home to millions and millions of evangelical Christians who believe the creation of Israel is a portent or sign that the Second Coming is imminent.

Leon Uris began each chapter of his book with a quote from the Old Testament. Whether we like it or not, religion does play a part in this issue. I descend from a long line of devout Christians, though I am now no longer a practising Christian. Maybe I listened to John Lennon's song 'Imagine' too many times. Maybe it was the likes of Christopher Hitchens pointing out such biblical quotes as Deuteronomy 21:18. Religious beliefs just faded. Nevertheless, I acknowledge the centuries of discrimination and persecution of Jewish people by Christians. That mistreatment was a powerful motivation for Jewish people to want to feel safe in a land of their own. But should one form of religious persecution be replaced with another?

Final Thoughts

ALTHOUGH THE SITUATION FOR THE PALESTINIANS REMAINS bleak, I feel satisfied that my shoe leather was not worn out in vain. Walking for Palestine did bring a lot of focus and attention to the issue. I believe in the political and human rights for Palestinians, the same way I believe in those rights for all human beings.

After the passing of Australian legislation enshrining marriage equality in December 2017, Penny Wong stated:

'Equality is a remarkably persistent principle. It is a defining principle. A principle that springs from the simple and powerful precept of the inherent dignity of every human being, and so it has been through history.'

That principle, so eloquently expressed by the good senator, is the same principle we seem to have applied to the Palestinian people, indeed all people in every corner of the globe.

Acknowledgements

IT IS NECESSARY TO MENTION A NUMBER OF PEOPLE WITHOUT whose support this book would not now be in your hands.

To my precious daughter Penelope, for initially suggesting I put pen to paper. By the way, no father has ever loved a daughter more than I have loved you.

To those who offered advice on, and suggested improvements to, the manuscript: Antony Loewenstein, Marcelo Svirsky, Bishop George Browning, Vacy Vlazna, Vivian Markham, Melissa Parke and Jessica Morrison.

To the many people who collected signatures for the two petitions I delivered to Canberra. Too many names to mention here, but I thank you sincerely.

To the many people, whose names I don't even know, who engaged with me whilst I was on the road. Your words of encouragement meant the world to me.

To the many people, in Australia and around the world, who have spoken out on this issue. Many of them Jewish. I salute you. Climate change may be the greatest existential issue of our time, but freedom for Palestine is surely one of the greatest moral issues of our time. It is not an easy cause to advocate for. Israel and her defenders will try to impugn false motives to you. A lack of tangible progress is no reason to diminish our efforts.

www.ingramcontent.com/pod-product-compliance
Lightning Source LLC
Chambersburg PA
CBHW041256040426
42334CB00028BA/3041